Penguin Handbooks

The Devon South Coast Path

Hugh Westacott was born in London in 1932 and moved to Epsom, Surrey, on the outbreak of the war. He was educated at Tiffin Boys' School, Kingston-upon-Thames, and the North-Western Polytechnic. He was for ten years the Deputy County Librarian of Buckinghamshire and has also worked as a librarian in Sutton, Croydon, Sheffield, Bradford and Brookline, Massachusetts. During the war he spent his holidays with his family in Colyton, east Devon, walking five miles to the sea and back again each day, and his love of walking stems from these experiences. He is now a freelance writer and lecturer and in 1979 he was commissioned by Penguin to write this series of footpath guides to every national park and official long-distance path. He has also written *The Walker's Handbook* (Penguin, second edition 1980) and two forthcoming books, *Long Distance Paths: An International Directory* and *The Backpacker's Bible.* His other interests include the history of the Royal Navy in the eighteenth century and the writings of Evelyn Waugh. Hugh Westacott is married and has two daughters.

Mark Richards was born in 1949 in Chipping Norton, Oxfordshire. He was educated at Burford Grammar School before training for a farming career. He discovered the pleasures of hill walking through a local mountaineering club. He became friends with Alfred Wainwright, the creator of a unique series of pictorial guides to the fells of northern England, who encouraged him to produce a guide to the Cotswold Way, which was followed by guides to the North Cornish Coast Path and Offa's Dyke Path. For two years he produced a selection of hill walks for the *Climber and Rambler* magazine, and more recently he has contributed articles and illustrations to the *Great Outdoors* magazine and numerous walking books, culminating in the present series of Penguin footpath guides. As a member of various conservation organizations and a voluntary warden of the Cotswolds Area of Outstanding Natural Beauty, he is interested in communicating the need for the protection of environmental and community characteristics, particularly in rural areas. Mark Richards is happily married with two lively children, Alison and Daniel.

The Devon
South Coast Path

H. D. Westacott

With maps by Mark Richards

Penguin Books

Penguin Books Ltd, Harmondsworth, Middlesex, England
Penguin Books, 625 Madison Avenue, New York, New York 10022, U.S.A.
Penguin Books Australia Ltd, Ringwood, Victoria, Australia
Penguin Books Canada Ltd, 2801 John Street, Markham, Ontario, Canada L3R 1B4
Penguin Books (N.Z.) Ltd, 182–190 Wairau Road, Auckland 10, New Zealand

First published 1982

Made and printed in Great Britain by
Richard Clay (The Chaucer Press) Ltd, Bungay, Suffolk
Set in Monophoto Univers

Contents

Acknowledgements

Many people have helped in the preparation of this guide. In particular I should like to thank John Heath for providing information on the state of the Path near Erme Mouth; R. H. E. Carter and the South West Way Association for help and advice; and the staff of the Devon County Library who provided so much information (it is fashionable these days to denigrate the work of local government officers, but there can be few organizations able to match the public library service for speed and efficiency). The faults are mine alone.

My thanks are again due to Mark Richards for the superb maps that are such a feature of the guide. The maps are based on the 1:25000 Ordnance Survey maps, with the sanction of the Controller of Her Majesty's Stationery Office (Crown copyright reserved).

And finally I must thank my daughter, Imogen, who typed the manuscript accurately and efficiently.

Although every care has been taken in the preparation of this guide, the author can accept no responsibility for those who stray from the right of way.

Introduction

The Devon South Coast Path (long-distance path A1d) runs for 143 miles from Plymouth to the Dorset boundary, just west of Lyme Regis. It forms part of the South-West Peninsula Coast Path (long-distance path A1), also known as the South-West Way, which follows the coast for well over 600 miles from Minehead in Somerset, via Land's End to Shell Bay in Dorset, just across the harbour from Bournemouth. The South-West Peninsula Coast Path is the longest path in Britain — more than twice as long as the Pennine Way (long-distance path D1). It has been devised and designated by the Countryside Commission and for much of its length follows the path patrolled by the coastguard until the outbreak of the First World War.

The Devon South Coast Path was created to enable long-distance walkers to explore and enjoy the magnificent scenery of this section of coastline. The first 7 miles to Turnchapel is almost entirely urbanized but will appeal to those interested in naval history. The 53 miles to Torcross (mile 60) is nearly all superb walking, though the next 7 miles of the route is on roads. Then follow 3 miles of good walking to Dartmouth (mile 70), but from Kingswear (mile 71) to Man Sands (mile 76) there are another 5 miles of road walking before resuming the Coast Path for another 4 miles to Brixham (mile 81). Now follow about 11 miles of mostly urban walking, often on roads, until, at mile 93, there are 6 miles of pleasant walking as far as Shaldon (mile 101). From Shaldon (mile 101) there are another 12 miles of urban road walking until resuming the Coast Path at mile 113 east of Exmouth. The rest of the walk is absolutely glorious and makes the duller sections seem worthwhile.

Long-distance paths were established for pleasure not for record-breaking purposes. Because our lives are governed by the need to conserve time, there is an unfortunate tendency to try to walk a route as quickly as possible. Unless you derive particular pleasure from testing yourself to the limit, take plenty of time and savour every moment of the walk. It is better to be able to laze on the beach or cliff top, enjoying the sun and the distant sound of the surf, to pass the time of day with other walkers, to watch the wildlife and examine the flowers than to have the nagging urge to keep going at all costs in order to keep to an unrealistically tight schedule. Experienced long-distance walkers know the value of Robert Louis Stevenson's much-quoted advice that 'To travel hopefully is a better thing than to arrive'. If you do not complete the whole route, you will not have 'failed' in any way at all, and there will be something to look forward to for another time.

It may come as a surprise to some to learn that parts of the Devon South Coast Path are very tough indeed and are as arduous as any part of the Pennine Way. A glance at the path profiles at the bottom of the maps will show that it is quite normal to have two or three very steep descents and ascents in the 3 miles or so covered by the page. Remember, too, that every ascent starts at sea level and goes to the top of the cliff, so there may be 1,200 to 1,500 feet of very steep climbing with the 3 miles. What goes up has to come down, so within the same distance will be a similar amount of descents and, as every experienced walker knows, coming down a steep hill is probably more tiring than climbing it, especially with a heavy pack.

Planning the Walk

When planning a walk along any long-distance path, the walker has to make two decisions which will affect the course of all his future actions. The first decision is in which direction to walk the Path. The second is whether to make a series of day excursions or to walk the route in one expedition on consecutive days. Most people walk from west to east (Plymouth to Lyme Regis), which means that they have the prevailing wind behind them.

On the whole, the length of the Path precludes most walkers from walking the Path in a series of separate days, spread over a period of time, unless they are fortunate enough to live fairly close to the route and are prepared to do a lot of driving.

The Path is very well served by public transport, with most of the towns and villages along the route having at least seasonal bus services. Outside the holiday season, some bus services are very much reduced or do not operate at all. Rail services are good, too. The start of the Path at Plymouth can be reached from all parts of the country by Inter-City expresses, and there is a bus service from Lyme Regis to Axminster from which the train can be taken to Exeter, Yeovil, Salisbury and London (Waterloo). In between there are railway stations at Kingswear (mile 71), on the privately owned Torbay Steam Railway, Paignton (mile 87), Torquay (mile 90), Teignmouth (mile 101), Dawlish (mile 105), Dawlish Warren (mile 107), Starcross (mile 109) and Exmouth (mile 111). Many points along the route are served, especially in summer, by long-distance express coach services.

Although much of the Path passes through magnificent coastal scenery, it has to be admitted that there are certain stretches which are so urbanized as to be scarcely worth walking and if time is pressing these sections can be omitted by using public transport. The 38 miles between Kingswear (mile 71) and Starcross (mile 109) is largely dull and urbanized, much of it over roads, with only one or two stretches of good walking:

Kingswear to Man Sands: 5 miles of inland road walking.

Man Sands to Brixham: 4 miles of good Coast Path walking.

Brixham to Broadsands: 4 miles of quite pleasant Coast Path walking.

Broadsands to Oddicombe: 11 miles, mostly on roads, and completely urbanized.

Oddicombe to Teignmouth: 7 miles of good Coast Path walking.

Teignmouth to Starcross: 9 miles, mostly urbanized, following the sea wall, the railway and roads.

A strong case can be made for taking the steam train (or bus) from Kingswear to Paignton and then bus or British Rail to Starcross (before booking the ticket, check that the Starcross ferry is operating – see p. 86).

Hazards and difficulties

Those who know the Devon coastline only from lazing on its beaches may be surprised to learn that they may encounter dangers along the route. One of the remarkable features of the Path is that considerable sections now lie beneath the sea! This is because many of the cliffs are subject to erosion and are constantly falling. Keep away from the cliff edge, or that splendid view may be your last, and on no account ever attempt to climb the cliff face as the surface is unstable and friable.

The line of the Path is usually clear, but walkers may experience some difficulty if a mist rolls in from the sea. No one who has not experienced this phenomenon can have any idea how frightening and disorientating it can be. Suddenly, and often with very little warning, the Path ahead disappears and all sense of direction is lost. On the less frequented sections the novice can find the experience alarming and chastening.

Gales, too, can be a hazard on the more exposed sections. A walker dressed in cagoule and overtrousers and carrying a large pack presents so much windage that at times it is difficult to keep a proper balance. I was once so frightened by the way that I was stumbling near the cliffs that I left the coast and retreated inland until the wind had moderated.

Perhaps a more welcome hazard (because it requires fine weather) is the risk of sunburn. On a fine day the walker will receive several hours' exposure to sunlight, which will be magnified by reflection from the sea. It is important to acclimatize slowly until a good tan has been acquired. Wind can burn the skin as painfully as can the sun and it is a good plan to carry some salve to help to prevent the lips from chapping and cracking. During the very hot summer of 1976 a number of walkers suffered from dehydration. Some actually had to be rescued on farm trailers and hosed down to restore their body fluids.

In dry weather the surface of the Path is likely to be firm, but after heavy rain some of the slopes on the steep hills will be slippery and treacherous.

Estuaries and ferries

Walkers should be aware that there are a number of estuaries and ferries which can present serious problems and delays. For example, anyone arriving at Erme Mouth (mile 26) in the early afternoon, having just missed low tide, will have to wait until the following afternoon before crossing or be prepared to get up in the middle of the night! This is because there is no ferry and no practicable crossing point for miles. Therefore it is important to know the times of low tide at Erme Mouth (mile 26) and Bigbury-on-Sea (mile 32) on the dates that you are likely to want to cross the river.

This can be done in the following way. Nautical almanacs give the times of *high* tides for every day of the year at certain selected ports. Other ports and estuaries are given tidal constants which can be added to the time of high tide at the port to which the constant refers. Thus, it is possible to establish the times of the tides for most resorts. Walkers are interested in *low* tides and these normally occur 6 hours and 10 minutes *after* high tide.

The two most used almanacs are Reed's *Nautical Almanac* and Brown's *Nautical Almanac*, which may be consulted at most good public reference libraries. The *approximate* times of tides can be obtained from the current edition of the AA *Member's Handbook*, which gives tidal constants in relation to London Bridge for one day of each week of the year. Most national newspapers publish the time of high water at London Bridge, but this is only of limited use for advance planning. Both Erme Mouth and Bigbury-on-Sea have the same tidal constant.

Almanac	Port	*Tidal constant for Erme Mouth & Bigbury-on-Sea*
Brown	Devonport	+0
Reed	Plymouth	+5 minutes
AA Handbook	London Bridge	+4 hours
Add 6 hours 10 minutes to establish time of low tide.		

The estuaries and ferries on the route are as follows:

Newton Ferrers (mile 14) across the Yealm: Seasonal ferry (see p. 32).

River Erme (mile 26): No ferry but normally fordable at low water (see p. 38).

Bigbury–Bantham (mile 31). Seasonal ferry and normally fordable in good conditions at low water (see p. 40).

Salcombe–East Portlemouth (mile 46): Ferry operates throughout the year (see p. 48).

Dartmouth–Kingswear (mile 70): Ferry operates throughout the year (see p. 62).

Shaldon–Teignmouth (mile 101): Ferry operates throughout the year (see p. 80).
Starcross–Exmouth (mile 109): Seasonal ferry. Not fordable (see p. 86).

Maps, timetables and accommodation

Although this guide contains all the information necessary to follow the route of the Devon South Coast Path, many walkers will want to arm themselves with additional information. It is very useful to have a map which sets the Path within the context of the surrounding countryside. Sheets 192, 201 and 202 of the 1:50000 Ordnance Survey map cover most of the Path except the last 6 miles from Seaton (mile 136), which is on sheet 193. The 1:100000 Bartholomew map sheet number 2, South Devon, covers the whole of the Path except for the last 16 miles east of Sidmouth (mile 125), which are on sheet number 4, Dorset. These maps lack some of the detail of the larger-scale Ordnance Survey maps, but the Coast Path is marked on them and they will be found to be perfectly satisfactory, saving both weight and money. Some walkers find that a cheap motoring map published by one of the oil companies is perfectly adequate.

Rural bus services are subject to change, withdrawal and reduction. Furthermore, some of them are seasonal, and any walker planning to use public transport will be well advised to obtain beforehand copies of the relevant timetables. The Devon edition of the Western National Bus Company contains details of all bus services (including independent operators) and train services within the county. It also contains timetables and details of ferry services which will be found to be invaluable. Price and postage are likely to vary from year to year, so blank cheques should be made out to the Western National Bus Company. Copies may be obtained from: The Western National Bus Company, National House, Queen Street, Exeter, Devon EX4 3TF.

For the whole length of this delectable coastline there is plenty of accommodation available. Outside the high season from mid-July to mid-September advance booking is not necessary, but do not expect to find vacancies in the busy holiday period. The South West Way Association has a useful accommodation list in its annual handbook (see p. 16). Accommodation lists published by commercial concerns, tourist boards and the publicity departments of local authorities can be consulted at most large public libraries throughout the country.

Youth Hostels are located at Plymouth, Bigbury-on-Sea (mile 31), Salcombe (mile 44), Start Bay (at Strete, mile 63), Maypool (between Kingswear (mile 71) and Brixham (mile 81) and some way off the Path) and Beer (mile 134).

Authorized camping sites are plentiful on the route of the Path. Walkers should note that they have no right to camp anywhere, not even on the beach, without first obtaining the permission of the landowner.

Kit and equipment

Experienced walkers know that there is nothing to beat well-broken-in boots for comfort on a long march. However, stout shoes with two pairs of socks will suffice. Track shoes and canvas boots are not suitable, especially if a heavy pack is being carried, as they may disintegrate on some of the steep hills.

In summer, wear cotton underclothes, breeches or loose cotton trousers and a cotton T-shirt or light woollen sweater. Shorts may be suitable in fine weather, but do beware of sun-burn and ensure a healthy tan *before* starting the walk. A cagoule and nylon overtrousers, if you have them, are useful for foul weather, but a plastic mac and overtrousers will serve. Do not wear jeans, as they are too tight and miserably cold and clinging when wet.

All gear should be carried in a comfortable, well-fitting ruck-sack.

Food and water

It is essential that all walkers should carry plenty of water, as many of the cafés are seasonal and may not be open. Water can be drawn from public conveniences, which are marked on the maps, and begged from cafés and public houses which you have patronized. If the loos do not have a drinking water tap, draw water from the wash basin and add some water-purifying tablets just in case it is not from the mains.

It is also wise to carry sufficient food to last for at least a day, and more if backpacking. The towns and villages which have grocer's shops are mentioned in the text.

How to use the guide

The purpose of this guide is to provide all the information that the walker requires to enable him to walk the route of the Devon South Coast Path, either from the east or from the west. The main body of the guide comprises 41 strip maps of the route on a scale of 1:25000 (approximately 2½ ins. to the mile) which show the route in very great detail, including information such as the location of gates, stiles, signposts and waymarks which the Ordnance Survey do not show on their maps. Although based on the Ordnance Survey maps (with the sanction of the Controller of Her Majesty's Stationery Office), they have been updated by means of personal survey and are thus more accurate.

A great deal of thought has gone into the design of the maps and they must be studied carefully in conjunction with the key in order to get the most from them. To reduce the amount of unnecessary detail and to avoid cluttering them unduly, contour and grid lines have been omitted. Instead, grid line numbers form the frame of each map, so that it is possible to relate them to any Ordnance Survey map and to use a compass, if required. Instead of indicating heights in the conventional way, a profile of the Path is shown in half scale at the bottom of every map. The numbers in the path profile relate to the mile numbers given on the map. In this way it is possible to see at a glance whether the section of the route to be walked is easy or strenuous.

It has already been said that the guide can be used in either direction. North, although always indicated, is of academic interest only and is not usually, on this route, at the top of the page. The guide is designed to be held in a natural reading position in front of the walker. Those travelling eastward towards Lyme Regis start at the front of the guide and their eyes follow the route *up* the page. Wayfarers travelling westward, towards Plymouth, start at the back of the guide and their eyes go *down* the page. The only disadvantage that those travelling west will be under is that the text will have to be read in reverse order (paragraph by paragraph, *not* word by word!).

Opposite every map is the relevant section of text. Here will be found brief notes of interesting things to be seen along the way and, wherever route finding is difficult, a description of the route to supplement the map. Information given in the text includes the location of shops, banks, post offices, cafés, restaurants, public houses and accommodation. Early closing days are given together with brief details of the availability of public transport.

Great care has been taken in the compilation of this guide, but walkers should be aware that the countryside is constantly changing and that time may render parts of this guide out of date. In particular, vandals may vent their wrath on waymarks and signposts. The author would be most grateful for comments and criticisms as well as information about changes which have made the guide out of date. (Please write c/o Penguin Books Ltd, 536 King's Road, London SW10 0UH.) Neither the author nor the publisher can accept any responsibility for the consequences incurred if the wayfarer departs from the right of way.

The South West Way Association

The South West Way Association was formed to promote the interests of users of the South-West Peninsula Coast Path, of which the Devon South Coast Path is a part. It invites all with an interest in the coast paths of the south-west to join.

The Association publishes a series of maps and guides to certain sections of the Path and an annual handbook somewhat misleadingly entitled *The South West Way: A Complete Guide to the Coastal Path.* It is *not* a complete guide in the sense that this guide is; nevertheless it is essential reading for anyone planning to walk any section of the Path, as it contains a large amount of up-to-date information about such things as temporary diversions, cliff falls, public transport, ferries and accommodation.

Inquiries about membership and the sale of publications should be made to: Mrs MacLeod, 1 Orchard Drive, Kingskerswell, Newton Abbot, Devon.

Tourist Information Centres

The Devon Tourism Office, County Hall, Exeter, tel. (0392) 53260, publishes information covering the county as a whole including lists of accommodation and campsites.

Local tourist offices provide similar information for their own area and are often in a position to offer helpful advice about accommodation. The following towns and resorts have information offices:

Plymouth: Civic Centre; tel. (0752) 68000 ex. 2309 and 2409
Salcombe: Market Street; tel. (054 884) 2736
Dartmouth: The Quay; tel. (080 43) 2281
Brixham: The Theatre, New Road; tel. (080 45) 2861
Paignton: Festival Hall, Sea Front; tel. (0803) 558383
Torquay: Vaughan Parade; tel. (0803) 27428
Teignmouth: The Den; tel. (062 67) 6271
Dawlish: The Lawn; tel. (0626) 863589
Exmouth: Manor Grounds; tel. (039 52) 3744
Budleigh Salterton: Rolle Street Car Park; tel. (039 54) 5275
Sidmouth: The Esplanade; tel. (039 55) 6441
Seaton: The Esplanade; tel. (0297) 21660
Lyme Regis: The Guildhall, Bridge Street; tel. (029 74) 2138

Geology

The geology of the south Devon coast is complicated. The main structure is composed of Devonian and Carboniferous rocks, which are sedimentary in origin and were formed under the sea. The Devonian beds were formed nearly three hundred million years ago and the different sediments have formed into layers or beds as a result of pressure. The oldest beds are the Dartmouth Slates which occur on either side of the Dart estuary, westwards to the Erme and Yealm estuaries and on both sides of Plymouth Sound. The middle layer, known as the Meadfoot Beds, can be seen around Torquay and in the South Hams, and the upper layer, or Staddon Grits, are to be found around Plymouth.

In some places the sedimentary rock has been overlaid with rock of organic origin. This includes limestone around Torquay (which is why there are caverns formed by the action of water), and volcanic ash at Hope's Nose and in Plymouth Sound.

Between Start Point and Bolt Tail is an outcrop of metamorphic rock consisting of fine-grained schists. East of Exmouth the rocks are of later origin — the characteristic red colour of the cliffs and soil is caused by the presence of red oxide of iron. These rocks are known as the New Red Sandstone. Towards the Dorset border is found limestone.

Between Plymouth and Berry Head is a series of rias or drowned valleys which give rise to the wonderfully lush scenery of which south Devon is so famous. Devonshire escaped glaciation during the Ice Age and consequently there are no significant lakes.

One of the curious features of the Devon landscape is the uniformity of the height and shape of the hills, most of which have flat tops. This phenomenon is thought to be caused by planation, when, during the Tertiary period about 70 million years ago, the land surface lifted and the relatively flat surface became eroded and finally tilted towards the south. During the Pleistocene period, about 2 million years ago, these planation surfaces were further eroded by rivers and the landscape assumed something like its present shape.

Book List

Guides to the Devon South Coast Path

Le Messurier, Brian, *The Devon South Coast Path*, HMSO, 1980.

Pyatt, E. C., *Coastal Paths of the South-West*, David & Charles, 1971.

South West Way Association, *The South West Way: A Complete Guide to the Coastal Path*, The South West Way Association, 1 Orchard Drive, Kingskerswell, Newton Abbot, Devon. (This annual publication is not a step-by-step footpath guide but a most useful compilation of essential information about accommodation, ferries, tides, cliff falls and diversions, etc. It should more properly be called a handbook.)

Ward, K., and Mason, John H. N., *The South-west Peninsula Coast Path*, Vol. 3, Plymouth to Poole, 2nd edn, Letts, 1980.

Westacott, Hugh Douglas, *A Practical Guide to Walking the Devon South Coast Path*, Footpath Publications, 1976.

General guides to Devon

Bates, Sir Darrell, *The Companion Guide to Devon and Cornwall*, Collins, 1976.

The Book of the Seaside, Drive Publications, 1972.

Burton, S. H., *Devon Villages*, Hale, 1973.

Chugg, Brian, *The Batsford Colour Book of Devon*, Batsford, 1976.

Delderfield, Eric R., *The Raleigh Country*, Raleigh Press, 1950.

Hammond, Reginald J. W., *The Complete Devon*, Ward, Lock, 1978.

Hunt, P. J. and Johnson, C. L., *Doorway to Devon*, Devon County Council, 1977.

Jellicoe, Ann, and Mayne, Roger, *Devon: A Shell Guide*, Faber, 1975.

Kay-Robinson, Denys, *Devon and Cornwall*, Bartholomew, 1977.

Mee, A., *The King's England: Devon*, Hodder & Stoughton, 1965.

Book List

St Leger Gordon, Douglas, *Devon*, 3rd edn, Hale, 1977.
Seymour, John, *The Companion Guide to the Coast of South-West England*, Collins, 1974.
Smith, Anthony, and Southam, J., *The Good Beach Guide*, Penguin Books, 1973.
Thompson, W. Harding, *Devon: A Survey of Its Coast, Moors and Rivers*, University of London Press, 1932.
Trewin, J. C., *Portrait of Plymouth*, Hale, 1971.
Westlake, Roy J., *View of Devon*, Hale, 1977.
Willy, Margaret, *The South Hams*, Hale, 1955.
Wonson, Mary Rowena, *Devon: Coast, Countryside, Forest and Moors*, Geographia, 1978.

Geology

Burton, S. H., *The South Devon Coast*, Werner Laurie, 1954.
Edmonds, E. A., *South-West England, British Regional Geology*, 3rd edn, H M S O, 1969.
Perkins, J. W., *Geology Explained in South and East Devon*, David & Charles, 1971.

Natural history

Barrett, J. H., and Yonge, C. M., *Pocket Guide to the Sea Shore*, Collins, 1960.
Beer, Trevor, *Devon's Animals of the Wild*, James Pike Ltd, 1975.
Beer, Trevor, *Devon's Birds*, James Pike Ltd, 1975.
Beer, Trevor, *Devon's Fossils, Pebbles and Shells*, James Pike Ltd, 1975.
Beer, Trevor, *Devon's Wild Flowers*, James Pike Ltd, 1975.
Burrows, R., *The Naturalist in Devon and Cornwall*, David & Charles, 1971.
Moore, Robert, *The Birds of Devon*, David & Charles, 1969.
Nature Conservancy Council, *Axmouth to Lyme Regis Undercliffs National Nature Reserve*, Nature Conservancy Council, 1977.
Wallace, T. J., *The Axmouth–Lyme Regis Undercliffs National Nature Reserve*, Allhallows School, 1963.

History

Andriette, E. A., *Devon and Exeter in the Civil War*, David & Charles, 1973.

Bradbeer, Grace, *The Land Changed Its Face*, David & Charles, 1973 (an account of the evacuation of part of the South Hams in 1943).

Chope, R. P., ed., *Early Tours in Devon and Cornwall*, David & Charles, 1967.

Collman, Morris, *Devon Long Ago*, James Pike Ltd, 1975.

Hoskins, W. G., *Devon*, David & Charles, 1972.

Hoskins, W. G., and Finsberg, R. P. H., *Devonshire Studies*, Cape, 1952.

Minchinton, Walter Edward, *Devon at Work, Past and Present*, David & Charles, 1974.

Minchinton, Walter Edward, *Industrial Archeology in Devon*, 2nd edn, Dartington Amenity Research Trust, 1973.

Pimlott, J. A. R., *The Englishman's Holiday: A Social History*, Harvester Press, 1976.

Russell, Percy, *A History of Torquay and the Famous Anchorage of Torbay*, Torquay Natural History Society, 1960.

Sellman, R. R., *Illustrations of Devon History*, Methuen, 1962.

Architecture

Laws, Peter, *A Guide to the National Trust Properties in Devon and Cornwall*, David & Charles, 1978.

Pevsner, Nikolaus, *The Buildings of England: South Devon*, Penguin Books, 1952.

Ships, smuggling and shipwrecks

Behenna, J., *West Country Shipwrecks. A Pictorial Record 1866–1973*, David & Charles, 1974.

Bouquet, M., *West Country Sail. Merchant Shipping 1840–1960*, David & Charles, 1971.

Boyle, V. C., and Payne, D., *Devon Harbours*, C. Johnson, 1952.

Coxhead, J. R. W., *Smuggling Days in Devon*, Raleigh Press, 1956.

Farquharson-Coe, A., *Devon's Smugglers*, Jarrold, 1975.

Farr, Grahame, *Wreck and Rescue on the Coast of Devon*, Bradford Barton, 1968.

Larn, Richard, *Devon's Shipwrecks*, Pan, 1977.

Phillipson, D., *Smuggling: A History*, David & Charles, 1973.

Folklore

Farquharson-Coe, A., *Devon's Folklore and Legends*, James Pike Ltd, 1975.
Farquharson-Coe, A., *Devon's Witchcraft*, James Pike Ltd, 1975.

Food and drink

Egon Ronay's Raleigh Pub Guide: Food and Accommodation, Penguin Books, 1981.
Lothian, Elizabeth, *Devonshire Flavour: A Devonshire Treasury of Recipes and Personal Notes*, 2nd edn, David & Charles, 1976.

Guide and Sectional Maps

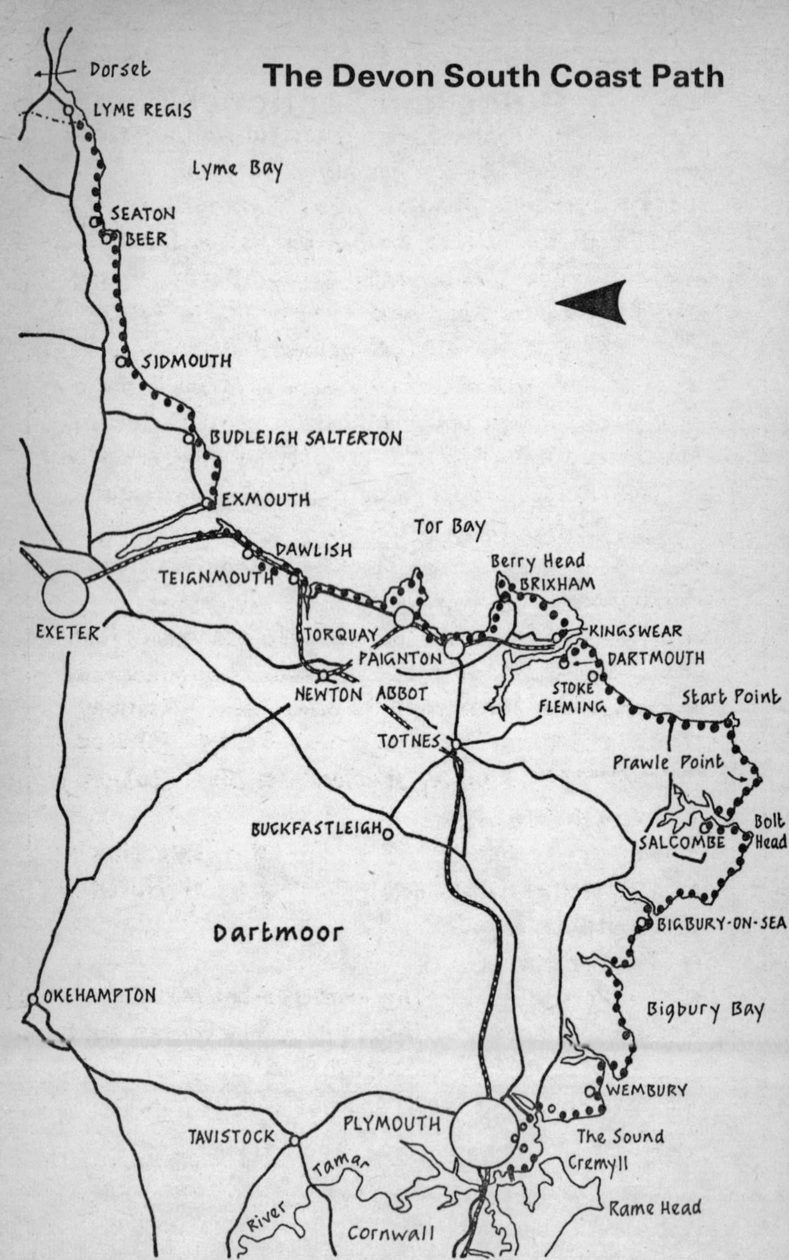

The Devon South Coast Path
Dorset
LYME REGIS
Lyme Bay
SEATON
BEER
SIDMOUTH
BUDLEIGH SALTERTON
EXMOUTH
Tor Bay
DAWLISH
Berry Head
BRIXHAM
TEIGNMOUTH
EXETER
TORQUAY
KINGSWEAR
DARTMOUTH
PAIGNTON
NEWTON ABBOT
STOKE FLEMING
Start Point
TOTNES
Prawle Point
BUCKFASTLEIGH
Bolt Head
SALCOMBE
Dartmoor
BIGBURY-ON-SEA
OKEHAMPTON
Bigbury Bay
WEMBURY
PLYMOUTH
The Sound
TAVISTOCK
Cremyll
Tamar
Rame Head
River
Cornwall

KEY

•••• Coast Path   °°°° Practical wading route
—— Coast Path on metalled surface
(31) Distance in miles from Plymouth
• • • • • Other visible paths or tracks
Hedge   Wall   Barbed Fence
Trees or Woodland   Plain Fence
Cliff or steep seaward slope
Low Water Mark (only shown at fordable estuaries)
High Water Mark
Marshy ground   Stream with direction
✛ Tumulus   Footbridge   of flow
Earthwork
✝ Church   ▲ Youth Hostel   Lighthouse or Beacon
Buildings (only shown to assist navigation)
WC : Public Conveniences   CG : Coast Guard Lookout Post
Major road   Minor road
Other road   Railway
Ferry service
Railway station   Bus station
C : Coast Path sign
B : Bridleway sign
D : Double (as in double gate)   Direction
F : Footpath sign   of North
FB : Footbridge
G : Gate   The numbers in the margin
K : Kissing Gate   locate the Northings and
S : Stile   Eastings (Grid Lines) on
W : Waymark   Ordnance Survey maps
17   17
05   04
Contour profile of route showing   91
milepoints and height in metres   31

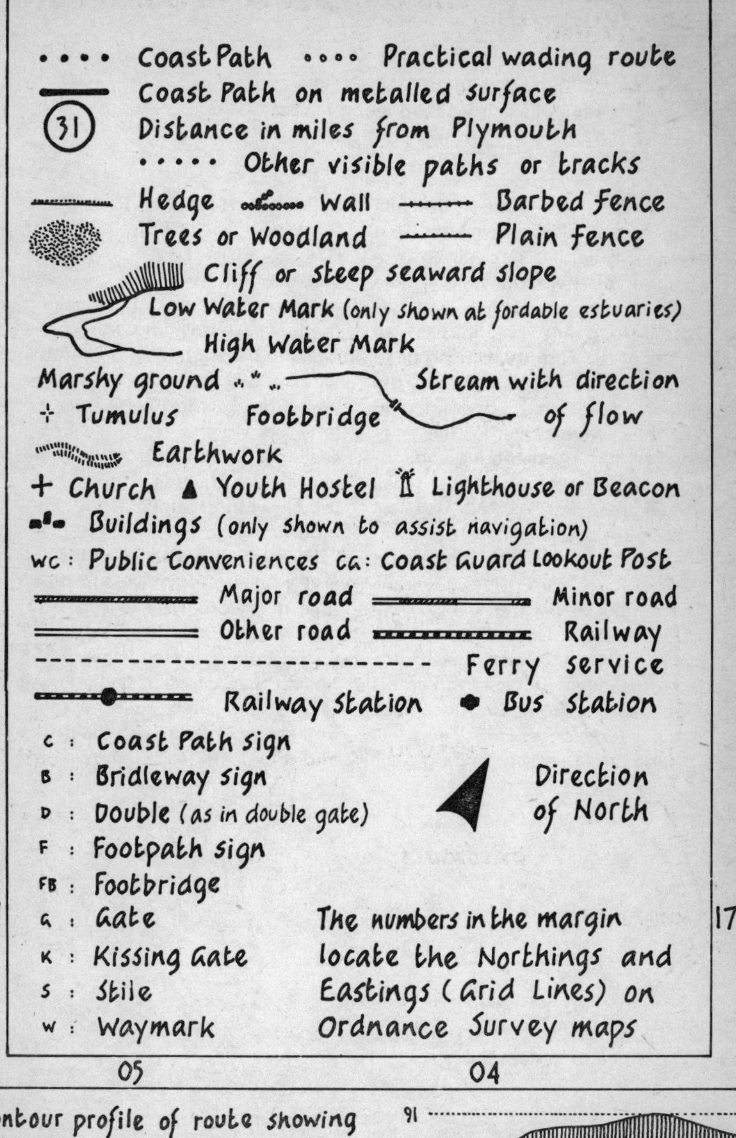

1. Plymouth

2 miles
Maps: 1:25000 sheet SX45; 1:50000 sheet 201
Terrain: Entirely urban walking along roads.

Plymouth, for most walkers the start of the long march, is a large city with a population of a quarter of a million. It is an excellent shopping centre and has good road and rail links to all parts of the country. Having been bombed very heavily during the war (more than a thousand people were killed), the city centre has been rebuilt and, although much of its old charm has been lost, most visitors will like its clean, bustling atmosphere.

The Cremyll Ferry landing at Admiral's Hard is generally reckoned to be the start of the Devon South Coast Path, as this is the point at which the South-West Peninsula Coast Path enters Devonshire from Cornwall. Although distances are measured from the Cremyll landing, the defined part of the Path starts from near mile 7 at Jennycliff Bay, south of Turnchapel. Most walkers will prefer to avoid 7 miles of road walking by taking the bus to Jennycliff Lane. Those walking the Path from September to May will have to start their walk from Newton Ferrers, as the ferry across the River Yealm is seasonal and there is no feasible alternative. There is a bus service to Newton Ferrers from Plymouth.

Walkers with a sense of history and a feeling for naval and maritime occasions may like to walk from Admiral's Hard and enjoy the views from the Hoe, one of the finest urban views in England. As well as the direct route, a more interesting one through the docks and round the Hoe is shown.

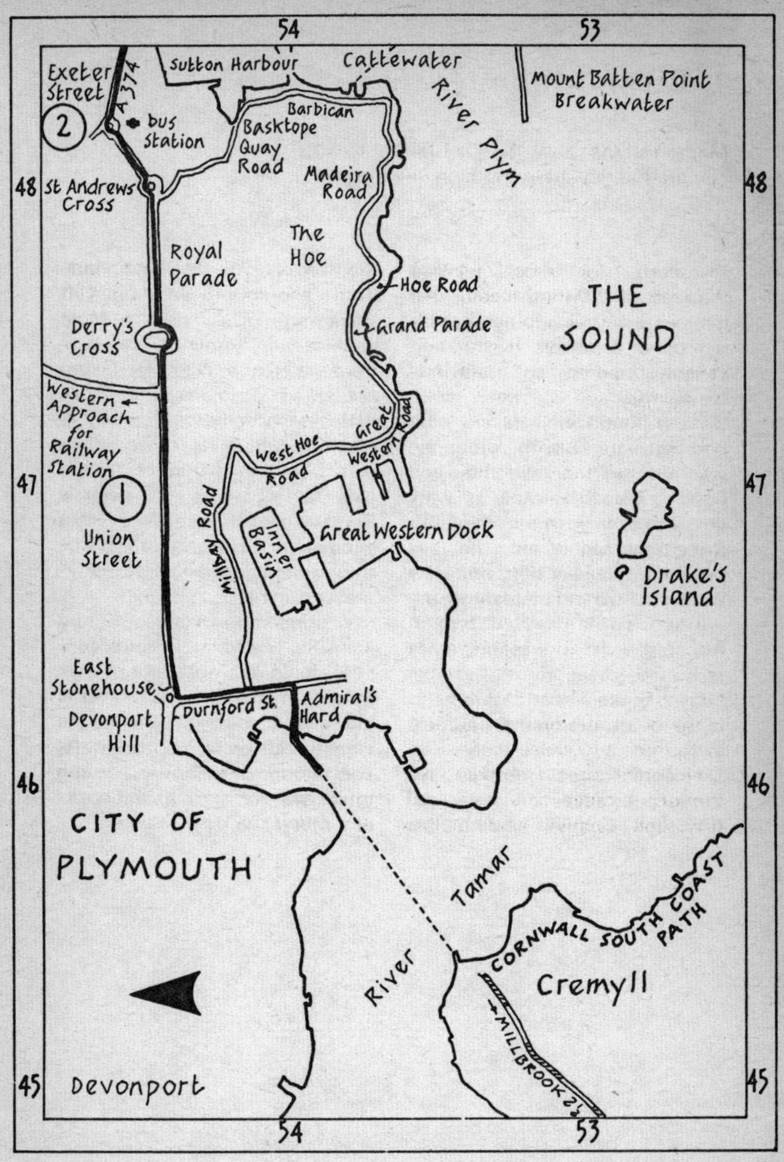

54
53
Exeter Street
A 374
Sutton Harbour
Cattewater
River Plym
Mount Batten Point
Breakwater
2
bus Station
Barbican
Basktope Quay Road
Madeira Road
48
48
St Andrews Cross
Royal Parade
The Hoe
Hoe Road
Grand Parade
THE SOUND
Derry's Cross
Western Approach for Railway Station
1
West Hoe Road
Great Western Road
47
47
Union Street
Millbay Road
Inner Basin
Great Western Dock
Drake's Island
East Stonehouse
Devonport Hill
Durnford St.
Admiral's Hard
46
46
CITY OF PLYMOUTH
Tamar
River
Tamar
CORNWALL SOUTH COAST PATH
Cremyll
MILLBROOK 2½
45
Devonport
45
54
53
Cremyll
River Tamar
15
1
2

2. Laira Bridge, Jennycliff Lane

5½ miles
Maps 1:25000 sheet SX45; 1:50000 sheet 201
Terrain: Urban walking mostly along roads, but with a short stretch through a park.

The path leaves the metalled road at Jennycliff Bay on a steep hill just below a small lay-by or passing place a couple of hundred yards or so from an acute left-hand bend.

West-bound walkers are now nearing the end of their journey. On reaching the road they will have to decide whether to walk the rest of the way into Plymouth along the road or take the Plymouth City bus from Jennycliff Lane into the city. Although the route round the Hoe and through the docks is interesting, with some fine views across the harbour, it is likely to appeal more to those setting out on their journey. In the last 140 miles those who have come from Lyme Regis have experienced such marvellous scenery that cities will seem dull in comparison.

Stanford Fort is now a holiday centre and country club, but 100 years ago was part of the defences to protect Plymouth from the French. These forts were known as 'Palmerston forts' or 'Palmerston follies'. In order to give the guns a clear field of fire part of the hill in front of Jennycliff Bay was pared to reveal a Romano-British cemetery. Other remains in the area of the RAF station date from 1000 B C.

In summer Jennycliff Bay (refreshments) can be reached by open-top bus from Plymouth (no. 53), which also goes on to Bovisand. Superb views can be had in the direction of Mount Edgecumbe and the Maker peninsula. The enormous blank wall is the safety wall of a nineteenth-century rifle range.

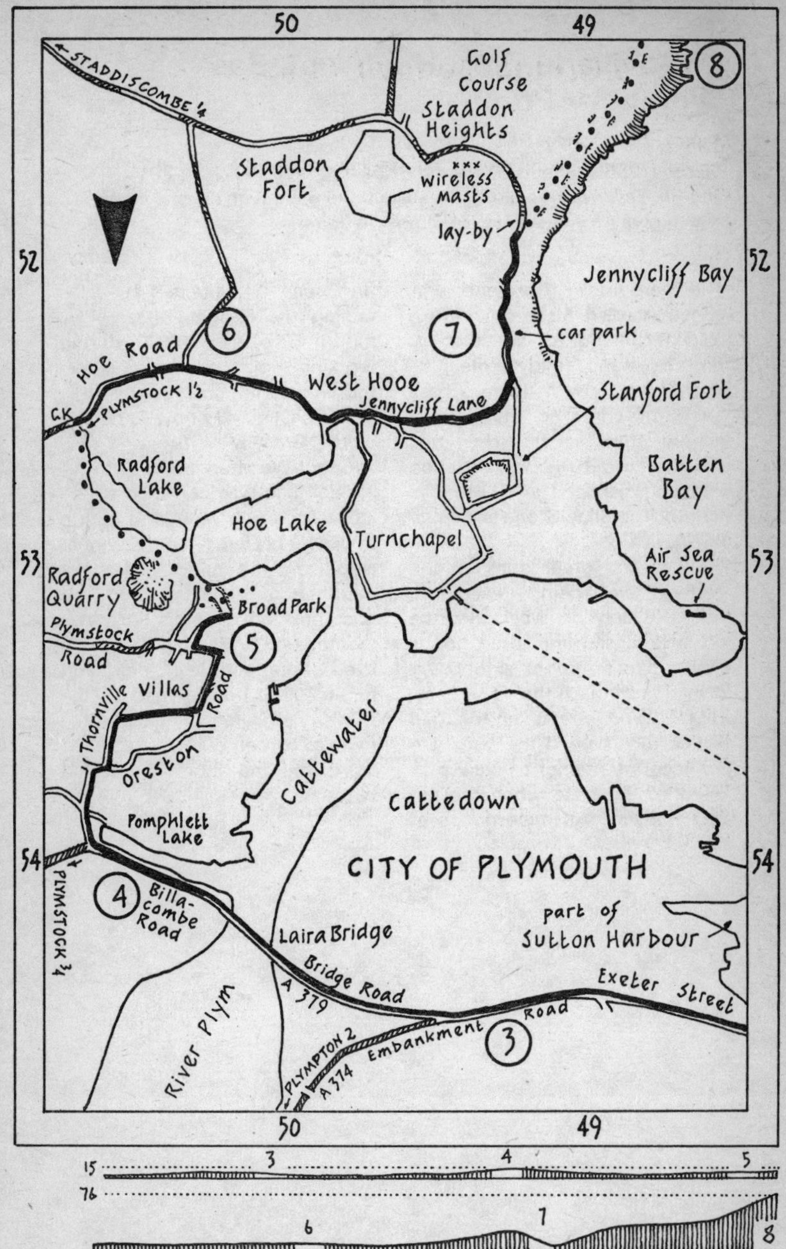

50
49
8
STADDISCOMBE 1/4
Golf Course
Staddon Heights
Staddon Fort
wireless masts
lay-by
52
52
Jennycliff Bay
6
7
car park
Hoe Road
PLYMSTOCK 1 1/2
West Hooe
Jennycliff Lane
Stanford Fort
C.K.
Radford Lake
Batten Bay
Hoe Lake
Turnchapel
53
53
Radford Quarry
Broad Park
Air Sea Rescue
Plymstock Road
5
Thornville Villas
Oreston Road
Cattewater
Pomphlett Lake
Cattedown
54
54
PLYMSTOCK 3/4
4
Billa-combe Road
CITY OF PLYMOUTH
part of Sutton Harbour
Laira Bridge
River Plym
Bridge Road
A 379
PLYMPTON 2
A 374 Embankment Road
Exeter Street
3
50
49
15
3
4
5
76
7
6
1
8

3. Bovisand Pier, Heybrook Bay, Wembury Point

3 miles
Maps: 1:25000 sheets SX45 and SX54/64; 1:50000 sheet 201
Terrain: Easy walking along a well-defined path, with coastal views which give a foretaste of the delights to come.

The harbour at Bovisand was constructed in 1816–24, with a reservoir inland, to service ships. Fort Bovisand (mid-nineteenth-century) is now a training base for under-water activities and a marine study centre. Heybrook Bay has a pub, accommodation and a bus service (no. 61) to Plymouth. The Shag Stone is directly out to sea.

When the great guns of the battery are being exercised, normally only on weekdays, the coast is closed and a red flag is flown. There is a signposted diversion through the naval base, H M S *Cambridge*, using the road which runs behind the guns. On no account attempt to walk seaward of the base when the red flag is flying. Advance notice of firing can be obtained by contacting the Range Officer (Plymouth 53740 ext. 412) during working hours or the Quartermaster at other times (ext. 406).

The best view is now to be had of the Great Mew Stone, a mile south of Wembury Point. In 1744 a local man was banished to the stone for seven years and built a house for his family on the gentler slope on the south side. His daughter remained, married and had three children. In the nineteenth century Samuel Wakeham lived there and kept pigs and poultry. It is now owned by the Ministry of Defence. Fulmars, kittiwakes and other sea birds breed there and the shore is infested with rats.

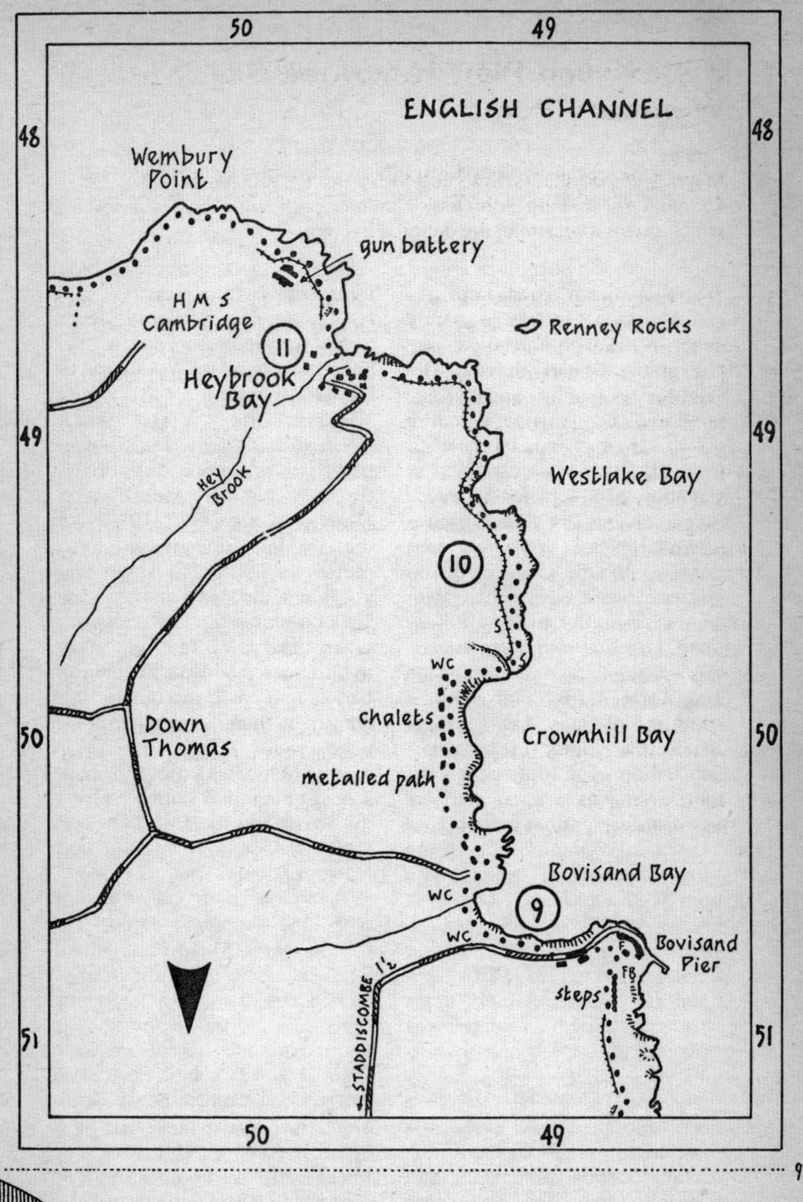

50
49
ENGLISH CHANNEL
48
48
Wembury Point
gun battery
H M S Cambridge
Renney Rocks
11
Heybrook Bay
49
49
Hey Brook
Westlake Bay
10
S
S
wc
chalets
Crownhill Bay
50
50
Down Thomas
metalled path
wc
Bovisand Bay
9
wc
Bovisand Pier
F
FB
STADDISCOMBE 1½
steps
51
51
50
49
91
9
10
11
15

4. Wembury, Newton Ferrers, Gara Point, Warren Cottage

5 miles
Maps: 1:25000 sheet SX54/64; 1:50000 sheet 201
Terrain: Easy walking along low cliffs and through a wood. There are fine coastal and estuary views.

Wembury has a post office stores, a public house, a café and accommodation. It has a sandy beach with a rich, inter-tidal variety of plants and animals. The Wembury Amenity Society has produced an illustrated nature trail guide which may be obtained from the National Trust shop at Wembury Mill, which also serves refreshments. The fifteenth-century church at St Werburgh faces the sea as boldly as any in Devon and contains a west gallery with an eighteenth-century balustrade, two fine seventeenth-century monuments to Sir John Hele and Lady Narborough and a painting of the Last Supper which is attributed to the Venetian School. The fourteenth-century tower was used by mariners as a landmark. Other buildings of interest in Wembury include the Hele Almshouses, which date from 1682 and have a chapel in the centre; Wembury Manor, which was built in 1591 and had a chapel added in 1682; and Wembury House, which dates from 1803 but which has terraces surviving from the sixteenth century.

Newton Ferrers has shops, a post office, a bank, cafés, the Dolphin pub on Beacon Hill, accommodation, a campsite and buses to Plymouth and Noss Mayo. Holy Cross church, rebuilt by Fellowes Prynne at the turn of the century, retains traces of early fourteenth-century work.

The ferry across the River Yealm (pronounced Yam) is seasonal and operates from May to September from 9 a.m. to 6 p.m. To attract the attention of the ferryman shout 'ferry', but it is even better to telephone beforehand to warn him of your coming (Newton Ferrers 872210). Note that the ferry operates on three routes, so tell the ferryman that you want the coast path. Those walking westwards out of season when there is no ferry will have to terminate their walk at Newton Ferrers and catch the bus to Plymouth, as there is no other practicable route.

Noss Mayo has a grocer's shop, a post office, two public houses, the Swan and the Old Ship, and a bus service to Plymouth and Newton Ferrers. There is a gently shelving beach at Cellar Beach where the swimming is good.

From Noss Mayo the path is wide, climbing past the former coastguard station to emerge into open country, the region known as the South Hams, above Gara Point. There is a fine view back towards the Cornish coast. Seals and porpoises can be seen off the coast in summer. This stretch is the so-called 'nine-mile drive' cut for Lord Revelstoke by local fishermen as an off-the-season job.

Look out for butterflies.

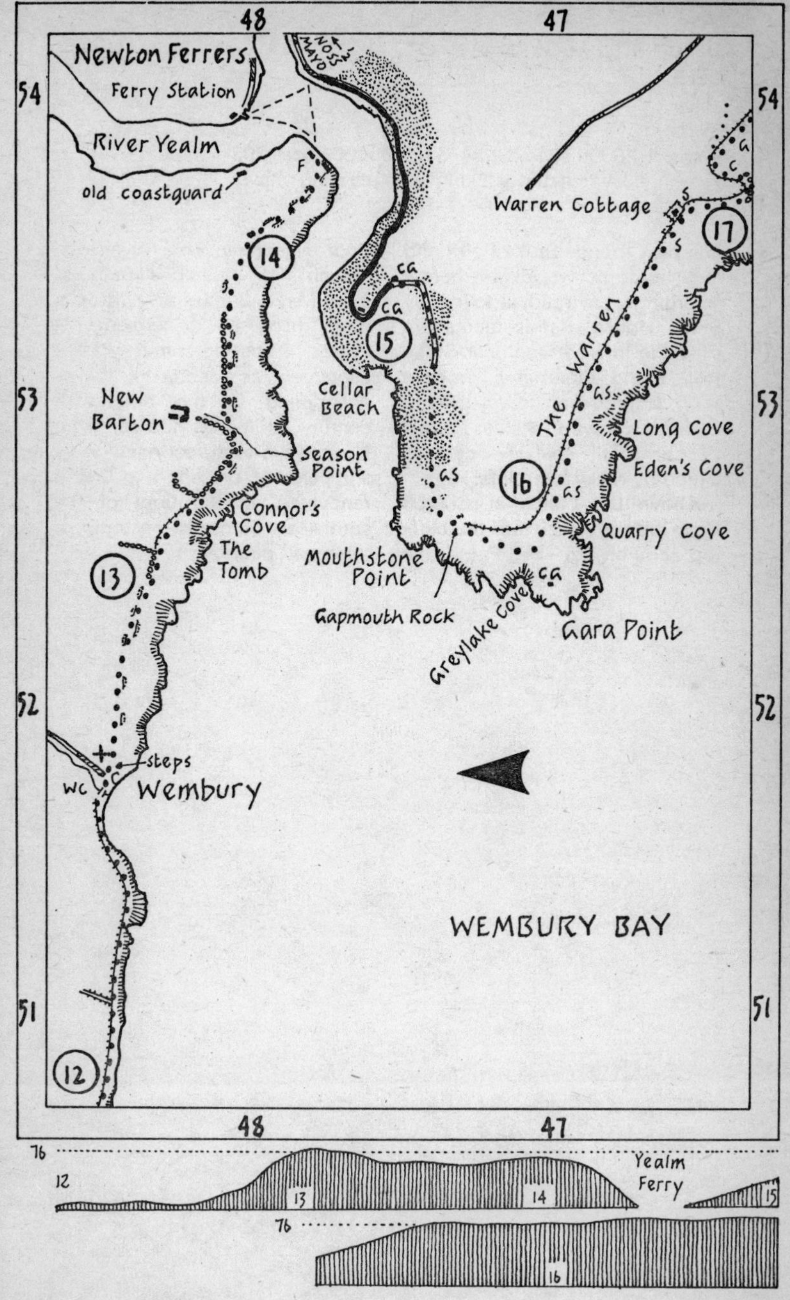

48
47
Newton Ferrers
NOSS MAYO
54
Ferry Station
River Yealm
old coastguard
F
14
Warren Cottage
54
S
17
CG
CG
15
The Warren
S
New Barton
Cellar Beach
GS
53
Long Cove
Eden's Cove
Season Point
16
53
Connor's Cove
GS
GS
13
The Tomb
Mouthstone Point
Quarry Cove
Greylake Cove
CG
Gapmouth Rock
Gara Point
52
52
steps
WC
Wembury
51
WEMBURY BAY
51
12
48
47
76
Yealm Ferry
12
13
14
15
76
16

5. Blackstone Point, Stoke Point, Row Cove

3¼ miles
Maps: 1:25000 sheet SX54/64; 1:50000 sheet 202
Terrain: Easy cliff-top walking with pleasing views.

The path rounds Stoke Point and runs through woodland before emerging at a road junction by Stoke House. Refreshments are available in a cottage near Stoke House and there is a grocer's shop. A track runs down through a large caravan site to Stoke Beach, small shelving pebbles edged by rocky low cliffs.

Above the beach at Church Cove are the remains of the cliff-top church of St Peter the Poor Fisherman (or Revelstoke church), the parish church of Noss Mayo, 2 miles away. It was often used by fishermen (St Peter, its patron saint, was a fisherman) as a landmark. It was abandoned in the nineteenth century as it was too far from Noss Mayo to attract many worshippers. At present it is being renovated. In the floor of the south-east corner is the tomb of a reputed pirate.

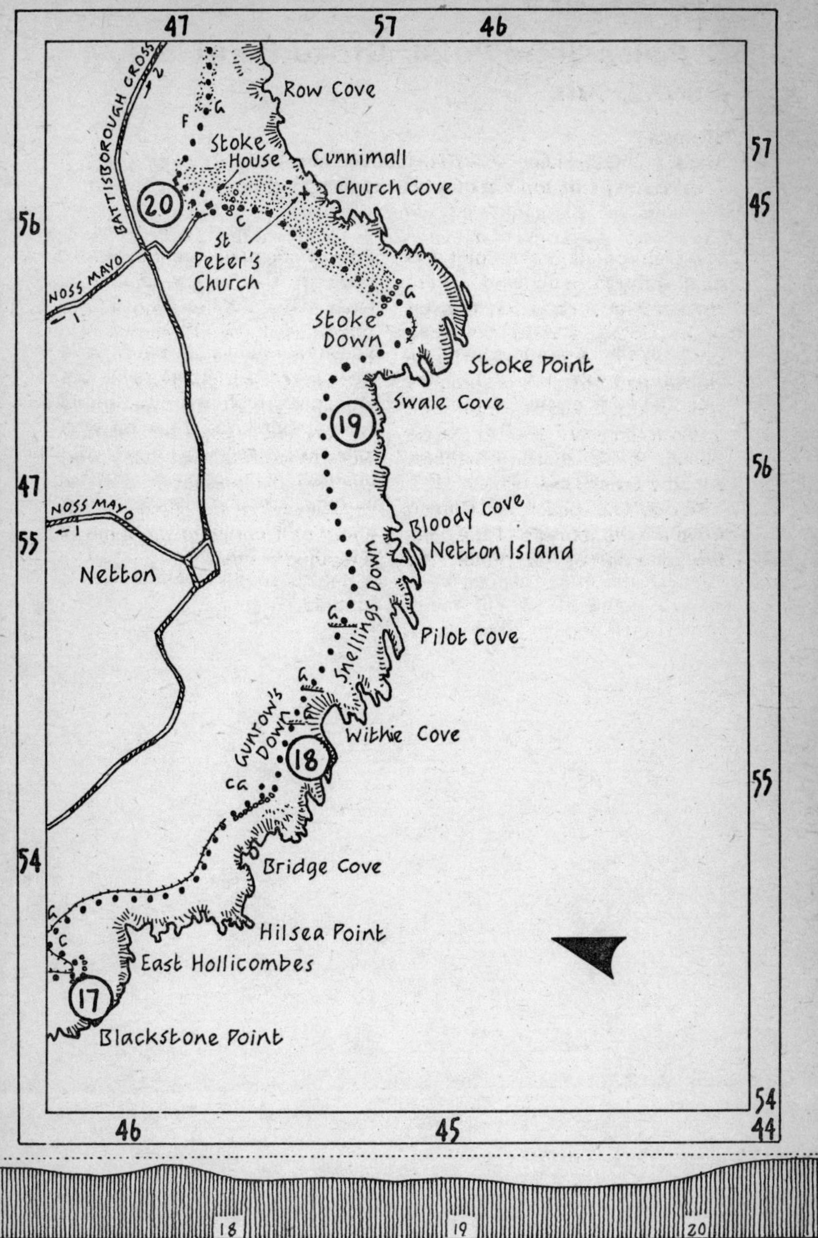

47
57
46
Row Cove
BATTISBOROUGH CROSS
F
G
Stoke House
Cunnimall
Church Cove
20
C
56
St Peter's Church
NOSS MAYO
1
G
Stoke Down
Stoke Point
19
Swale Cove
47
55
NOSS MAYO
1
Netton
Bloody Cove
Netton Island
Snellings Down
Pilot Cove
G
G
Gunrow's Down
18
Withie Cove
CG
54
Bridge Cove
Hilsea Point
C
East Hollicombes
17
Blackstone Point
46
45
57
45
56
55
54
44
18
19
20

6. Piskey's Cove, St Anchorite's Rock, Bugle Hole

3 miles
Maps: 1:25000 sheet SX54/64; 1:50000 sheet 202
Terrain: The path profile at the bottom of the map shows east-bound wayfarers that this is the first typically hilly section of their journey. Those who have come from Lyme Regis know that this is but a foretaste of some of the delights to come and regard this section as relatively easy.

The path climbs to the summit of Beacon Hill, on which can be seen the ruin of the Membland Pleasure House, recorded on an early map of 1765. It then drops downhill past St Anchorite's Rock, a massive tor 30 ft high which is a favourite perch for raptors. I have been unable to establish the origin of the rock's unusual name. It is not mentioned in the English Place-Name Society volume dealing with Devon and all other references to it give no hint of its origin. An anchorite was a person who foreswore the secular life in favour of a solitary life of prayer, fasting, mortification and silence, and it may be that such a person chose this spot for his cell.

Battisborough House is now a school.

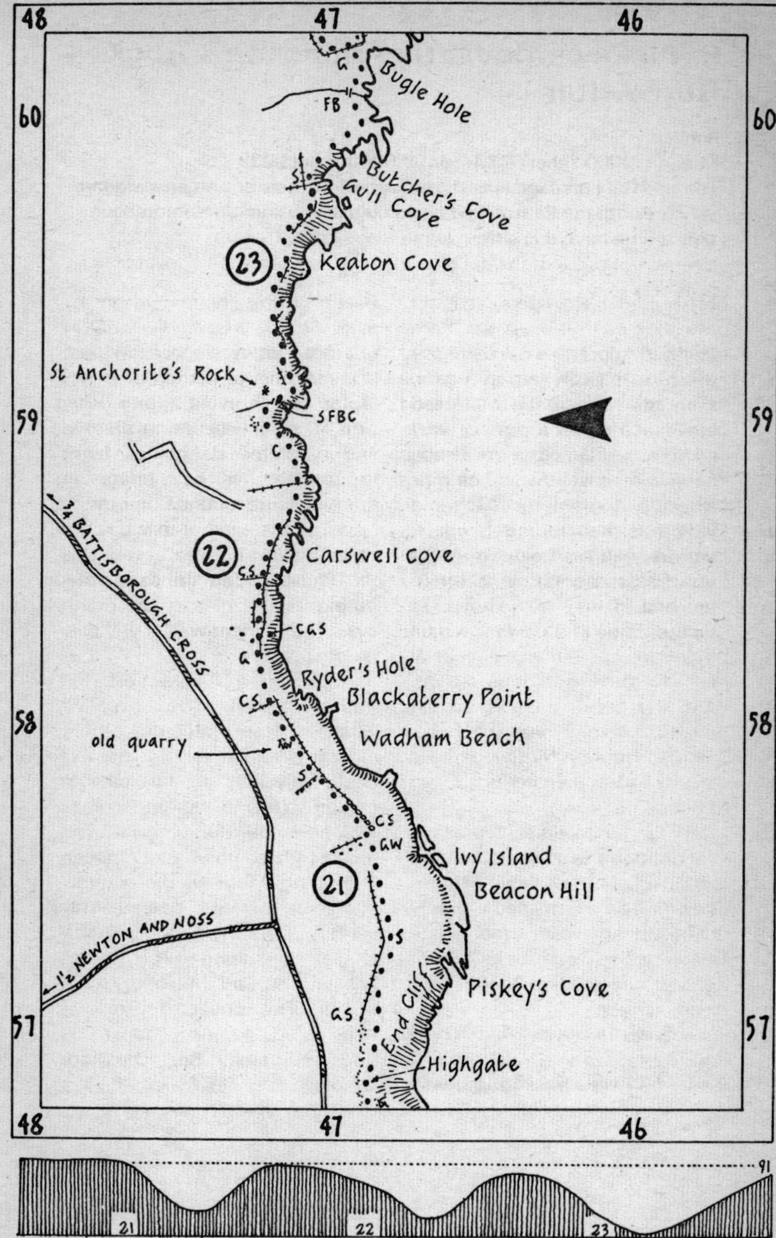

48
47
46
60
60
Bugle Hole
G
FB
Butcher's Cove
S
Gull Cove
23
Keaton Cove
St Anchorite's Rock
SFBC
59
59
C
¾ BATTISBOROUGH CROSS
22
Carswell Cove
C.S.
CGS
G
Ryder's Hole
C.S.
Blackaterry Point
58
Wadham Beach
58
old quarry
S
C S
GW
Ivy Island
21
Beacon Hill
1½ NEWTON AND NOSS
S
Piskey's Cove
GS
End Cliff
57
57
Highgate
48
47
46
91
21
22
23

7. Mothecombe, Erme Mouth, Freshwater

4½ miles
Maps: 1:25000 sheet SX54/64; 1:50000 sheet 202
Terrain: After an inland stretch through Mothecombe and an awkward river crossing, the Path follows field edges. The section from Beacon Point to Freshwater is strenuous.

East-bound wayfarers should note that on this map the Path begins at grid line 47. Where the Path turns sharply left, at a gate, to turn inland there is a well-used path which is not a right of way and which emerges at the beach at a gate near a slipway. The official Path turns left, follows a fence and then turns left again. Keep the hedge on your right for three fields and continue on to the road. Turn right at the T-junction. Devon County Council hoped to open the old coastal path but have not done so yet. From the beach there is a clear path to the road near the Erme. The road through Mothecombe is narrow and in summer is subject to heavy traffic.

Refreshments are served at the Old School and accommodation is available in the village. Mothecombe has remained totally unspoiled because the Flete Estate who own it have not allowed any development to take place.

Crossing the river Erme: There is no ferry and it is necessary to wade the river across to Wanwell Beach on the line shown on the map. *This is practicable only at one hour either side of low tide.* It is essential to plan your arrival at low tide to avoid a long delay or a 10 mile walk along narrow, and in summer dangerous, lanes to cross the river by a bridge on the A379. Instructions on how to calculate the time of low tide are given on p. 11. Even at low tide the crossing can be dangerous during heavy rain or in rough seas. The prudent walker will take no chances!

Holbeton, 1½ miles off the Path, is an attractive unspoiled village. The fifteenth-century church is remarkable for the exceptionally rich and fine carving on the sixteenth-century screens which divide the chapels. The nineteenth-century rood screen is a faithful copy of the original, and there is a fine seventeenth-century monument in the north chapel depicting 22 figures kneeling around the effigy of a knight. The public house was once a workhouse, hence its unusual name, the Dartmoor Union.

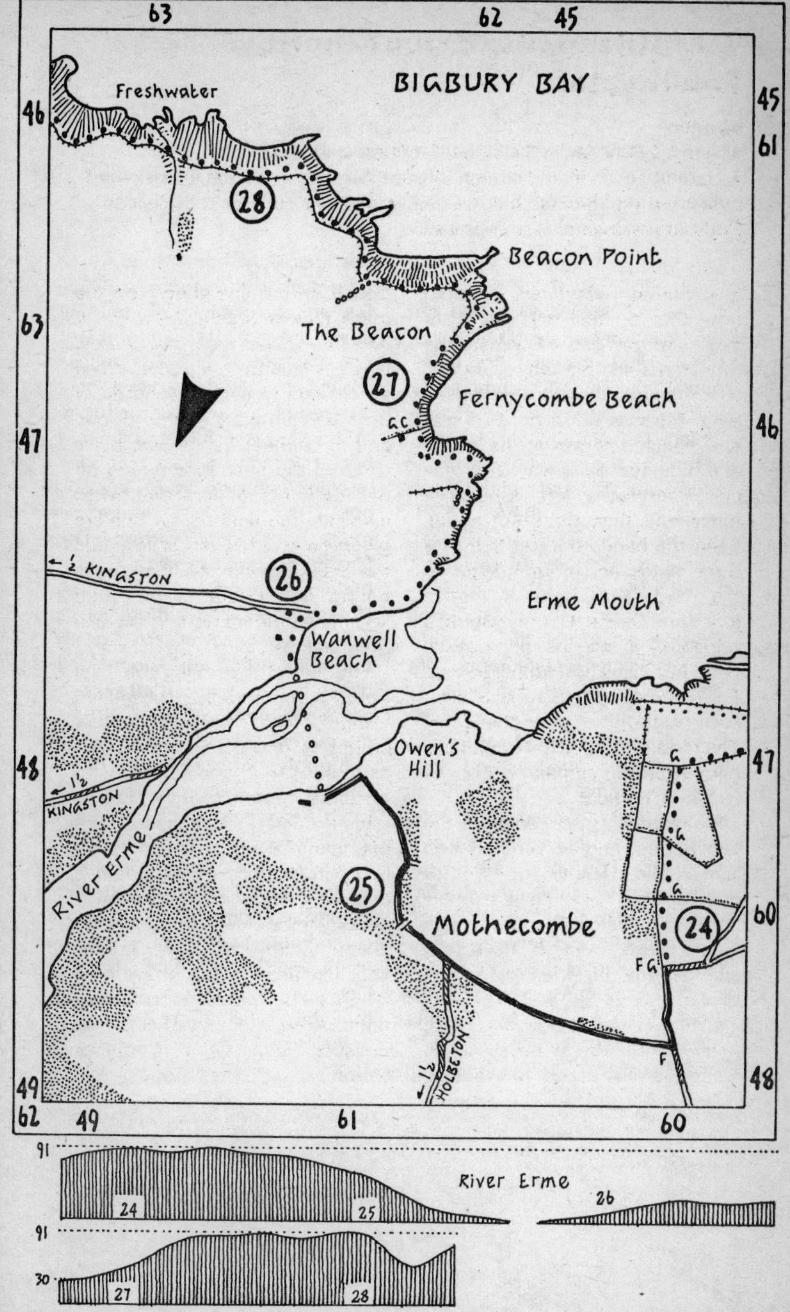

63
62
45
BIGBURY BAY
45
46
Freshwater
61
28
Beacon Point
63
The Beacon
27
Fernycombe Beach
G.C
47
46
½ KINGSTON
26
Erme Mouth
Wanwell
Beach
Owen's
Hill
G
48
47
½
KINGSTON
G
River Erme
25
G
Mothecombe
24
60
F G
49
F
48
62
49
61
60
91
River Erme
24
25
26
91
30
27
28

8. Hoist Point, Bigbury-on-Sea, Bantham Sand

3 miles
Maps: 1:25000 sheet SX54/64; 1:50000 sheet 202
Terrain: There are some steep gradients before reaching the seaside resort of Bigbury-on-Sea.

The path runs very close to the cliff edge, with some steep gradients, especially in and out of Westcombe Beach. Challaborough has a grocer's shop, cafés, public houses, accommodation and a campsite. There is a sandy beach, but bathing can be dangerous. In the charming village of Ringmore ($\frac{1}{2}$ mile) is the fourteenth-century Journey's End (recommended by Egon Ronay), where R. C. Sherriff wrote his famous play.

Bigbury-on-Sea has food shops, a post office, public houses, cafés, restaurants, accommodation, a campsite, a Youth Hostel and buses to Modbury (summer only) and Plymouth (bank holidays and Sundays in summer). At high tide an extraordinary tracked vehicle on stilts operates between the mainland and Burgh Island, from where it is worth visiting the ancient Pilchard Inn.

Walkers should time their arrival to take advantage of low tide so that they can cross the River Avon (or Aune). In summer months there is a ferry, but it operates only from Mondays to Saturdays in the months June to September (occasionally at other times) from 10–11 a.m. and 3–4 p.m. (Saturdays 2–3 p.m. and 5–6 p.m.). In July and August there is a Sunday service, but the future of this ferry is in doubt. If it is not operating and the tide has been missed the only practicable alternative is an 8-mile detour on roads via Aveton Gifford. The ferry is operated from the fourth building opposite in Bantham (Kingsbridge 3278). Shout 'ferry'. At low tide it is easier to reach the ferry crossing along the beach. *On no account attempt to cross the mouth of the Avon, as the current is very strong.*

Bigbury, one mile inland, has a church with a steeple dedicated to St Lawrence which, although virtually rebuilt in 1872, contains an early fourteenth-century sedilia and piscina, a fine lectern and pulpit, and some good fifteenth-century brasses. Bigbury Court, to the west of the church, is late-Georgian with much older outbuildings, including a circular dovecot.

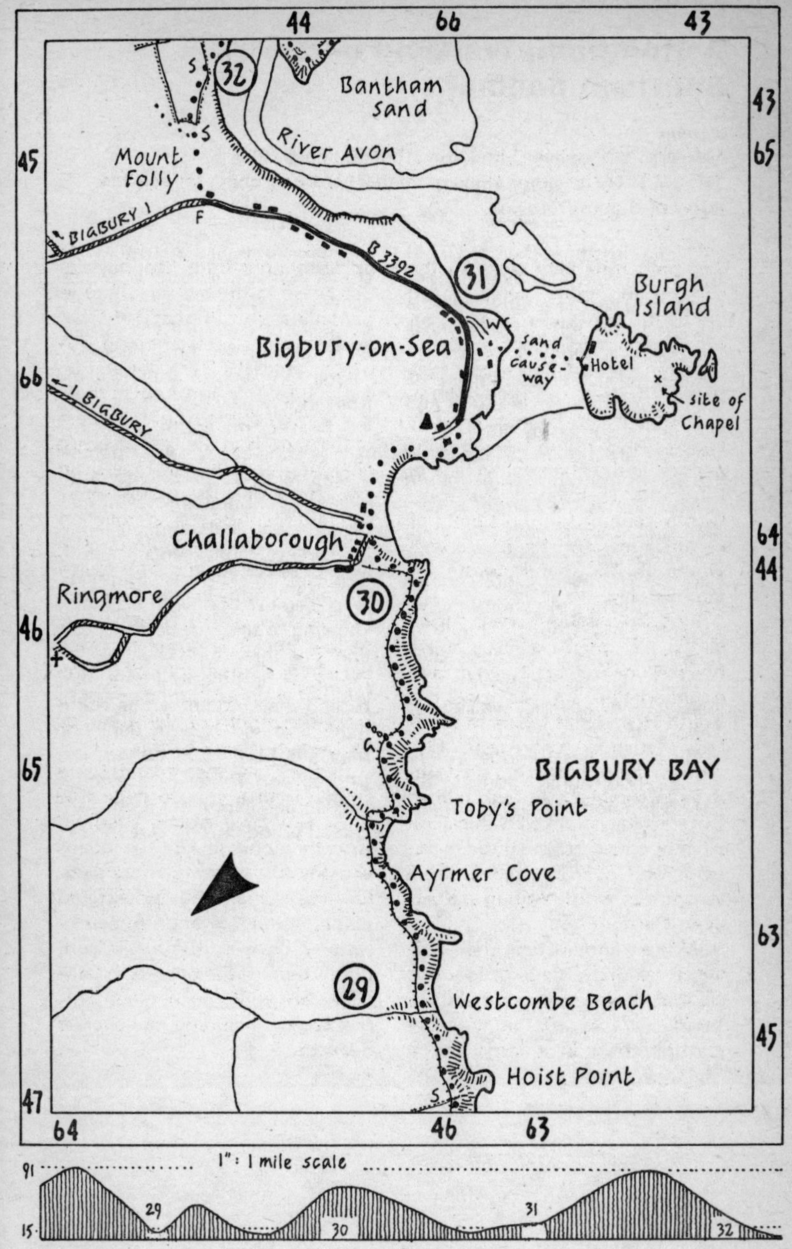
44
66
43
32
Bantham
Sand
S
River Avon
43
45
65
Mount
Folly
S
F
BIGBURY 1
B 3392
31
Burgh
Island
66
I BIGBURY
Bigbury-on-Sea
W
sand
cause-
way
Hotel
site of
Chapel
Challaborough
64
44
Ringmore
30
46
G
65
BIGBURY BAY
Toby's Point
Ayrmer Cove
63
Westcombe Beach
29
45
Hoist Point
S
47
64
46
63
1": 1 mile scale
91
29
31
15
30
32

9. Bantham, Warren Point, Thurlestone Sands

4 miles
Maps: 1:25000 sheet SX54/64; 1:50000 sheet 202
Terrain: Pleasant, easy walking.

Walkers must time their arrival at Bantham to take advantage of low tide. There *is* a ferry, but it is seasonal and erratic (for details see previous page). Only attempt to take a short cut across the Avon (or Aune) at low tide and on the line shown by dots. *On no account attempt to take a short cut across the sands at the mouth of the river as the current is very fast and dangerous.* The path continues on the seaward boundary of Thurlestone golf course for $1\frac{1}{4}$ miles. A short detour around Links Court, a block of flats, is optional, because of a landslip, but the South West Way Association advises walkers to keep to the path.

Bantham has a post office stores, two public houses, the Sloop Inn and the Old Ship, and a restaurant.

Thurlestone has a post-office stores, a café, a public house, accommodation and buses to Kingsbridge and Inner Hope. Early closing is on Thursdays. Thurlestone, which gets its name from the wave-cut arch (a thirle is a hole) at the south end of the bay, is an exceptionally attractive village, with a fine church dedicated to All Saints. It has an unusual tower and contains some interesting monuments, including one to Thomas Stephens, who died in 1658, with his family kneeling in the Elizabethan tradition. The three sons kneel behind the father and the four daughters behind their mother, while above them is a red bundle depicting their still-born child on his way to heaven. There is a circular sandstone Norman font and carved wooden rood screen.

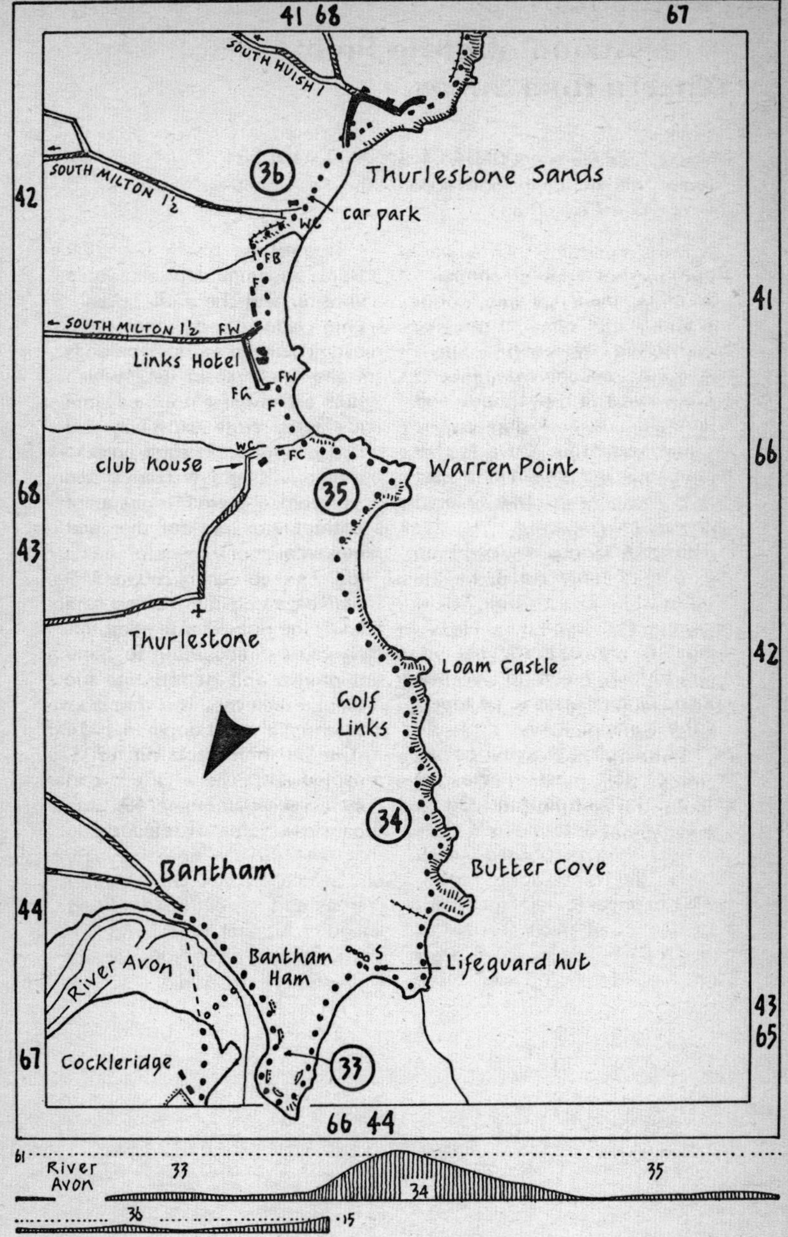

SOUTH HUISH 1
SOUTH MILTON 1½
36
Thurlestone Sands
car park
WC
FB
F
← SOUTH MILTON 1½
FW
Links Hotel
FW
FG
F
WC
club house →
FC
35
Warren Point
Thurlestone
Loam Castle
Golf Links
34
Bantham
Butter Cove
River Avon
Bantham Ham
S
Lifeguard hut
Cockleridge
33
66 44
River Avon
61
33
34
35
36
·15

10. Beacon Point, Hope Cove, Bolt Tail, Lantern Rock

4 miles
Maps: 1:25000 sheet SX54/64; 1:50000 sheet 202
Terrain: This section includes some of the most spectacular walking on the whole Coast Path.

Hope Cove has food shops, a post office, the Hope and Anchor Inn and the Lobster Pot Inn (recommended by Egon Ronay), restaurants, accommodation and a bus service to Kingsbridge and Salcombe. Early closing day is Wednesdays. Hope Cove is very picturesque and is seen at its best out of season – at other times it gets very crowded.

The path climbs steeply from the road in Inner Hope, by the Methodist chapel, to Bolt Tail, a popular beauty spot, but once beyond it the crowds are left behind.

An Iron Age cliff fort with a noticeable rampart is to be found on the summit. It was probably part of a larger site. Now comes some of the most spectacular cliff-top walking on the South Coast. The rock formations consist of metamorphosed mica schists, the older rock having been changed under high pressure. Flakes of mica crystals of quartz can be clearly seen. Port Light has a public house serving meals, accommodation and a campsite, and there are refreshments facilities by the radio masts. This whole stretch belongs to the National Trust, which issues a pamphlet on local flora and fauna. Note especially the shags, fulmars, greater black-backed gulls and buzzards, and apart from a plentiful spread of sea thrift look out for the rarer blue vernal squill.

On 15 February 1760, HMS *Ramillies*, an 82-gun second-rate ship of the line, was wrecked off Bolt Tail (or, according to some authorities, Bolt Head), with the loss of 800 lives. The *Ramillies* was originally laid down in 1644 as the *Katherine*, rebuilt in 1702, renamed *Ramillies* in 1706, and rebuilt yet again in 1749. She took part in the ill-fated battle that lost Britain Minorca in 1756 and which resulted in the court martial and execution by firing squad of Admiral John Byng, 'To encourage the others', as Voltaire sardonically remarked.

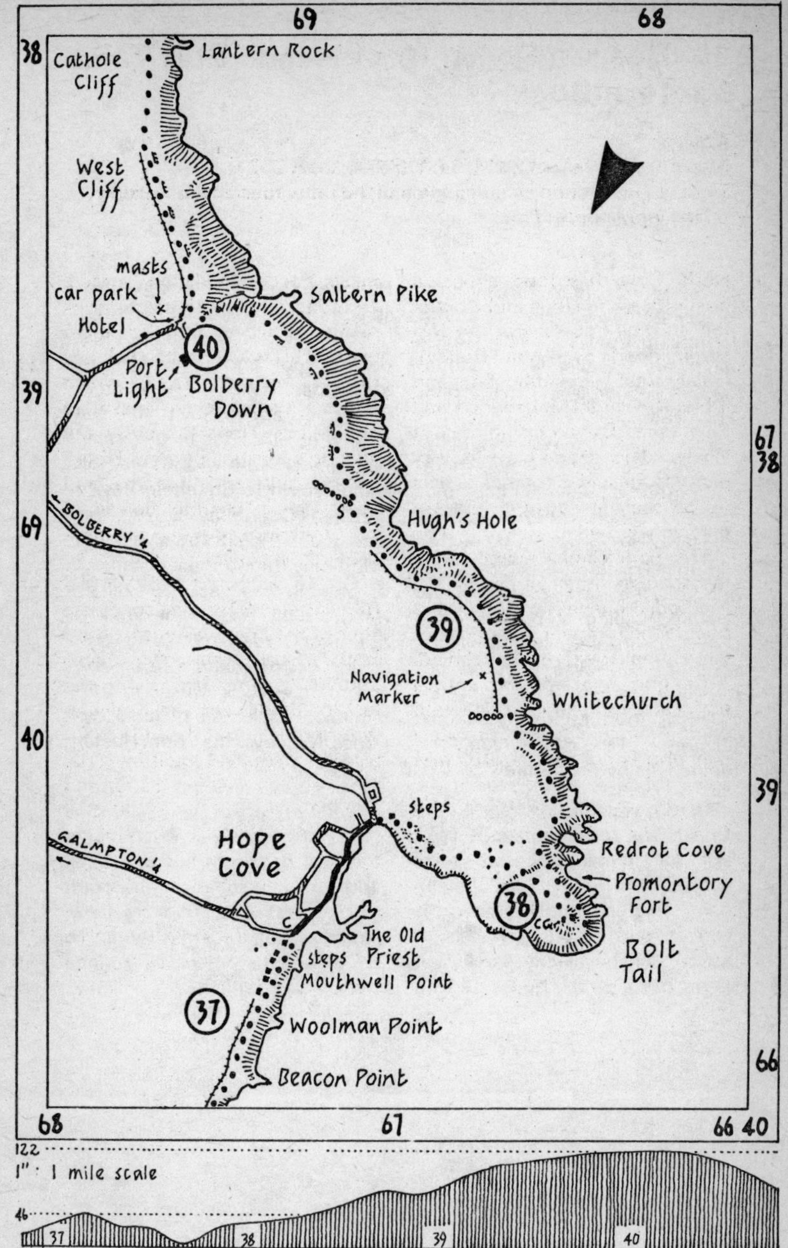
69
68
38
Lantern Rock
Cathole Cliff
West Cliff
masts
car park
Hotel
x
Saltern Pike
40
Port Light
Bolberry Down
39
67
38
BOLBERRY 1/4
69
Hugh's Hole
S
39
Navigation Marker
x
Whitechurch
40
39
GALMPTON 1/4
steps
Hope Cove
Redrot Cove
Promontory Fort
C
38
CG
Bolt Tail
The Old Priest
steps
Mouthwell Point
37
Woolman Point
Beacon Point
66
68
67
66 40
122
1": 1 mile scale
46
37
38
39
40

11. Soar Mill Cove, Bolt Head, Stink Cove

4 miles
Maps: 1:25000 sheet SX73; 1:50000 sheet 202
Terrain: Another very strenuous section, but after rounding Bolt Head the Path descends towards Salcombe.

By following the well-used but steeply sloping path inland along the stream from Soar Mill Cove, the weary traveller will reach a road, the Soar Mill Cove Hotel and a campsite.

Soar Mill Cove was originally known as Sewer Mill Cove. There is a nature trail between here and Bolberry Down approximately a mile long, organized jointly by the National Trust and Shell. In 1936 one of the last commercially operated sailing ships, the Finnish four-masted barque *Herzogin Cecilie*, was wrecked on the Ham Stone.

This is an exceptionally beautiful stretch of the Path which, fortunately, is owned entirely by the National Trust and is thus preserved for the nation for ever.

Bolt Head is another popular beauty spot and is a maze of footpaths. There is now more than one path to Salcombe, but follow the cliff edge to Bolt Head (signposted South Sands via Bolt Head) down to Starehole Bay to join the Courtenay Drive. This was constructed by Viscount Courtenay during the last century to provide easy access to Bolt Head. At the end of the Walk is Sharpitor Gardens, with a fine collection of roses and rare shrubs, and the Overbeck Museum, containing a collection of local bygones. Near by is the Youth Hostel.

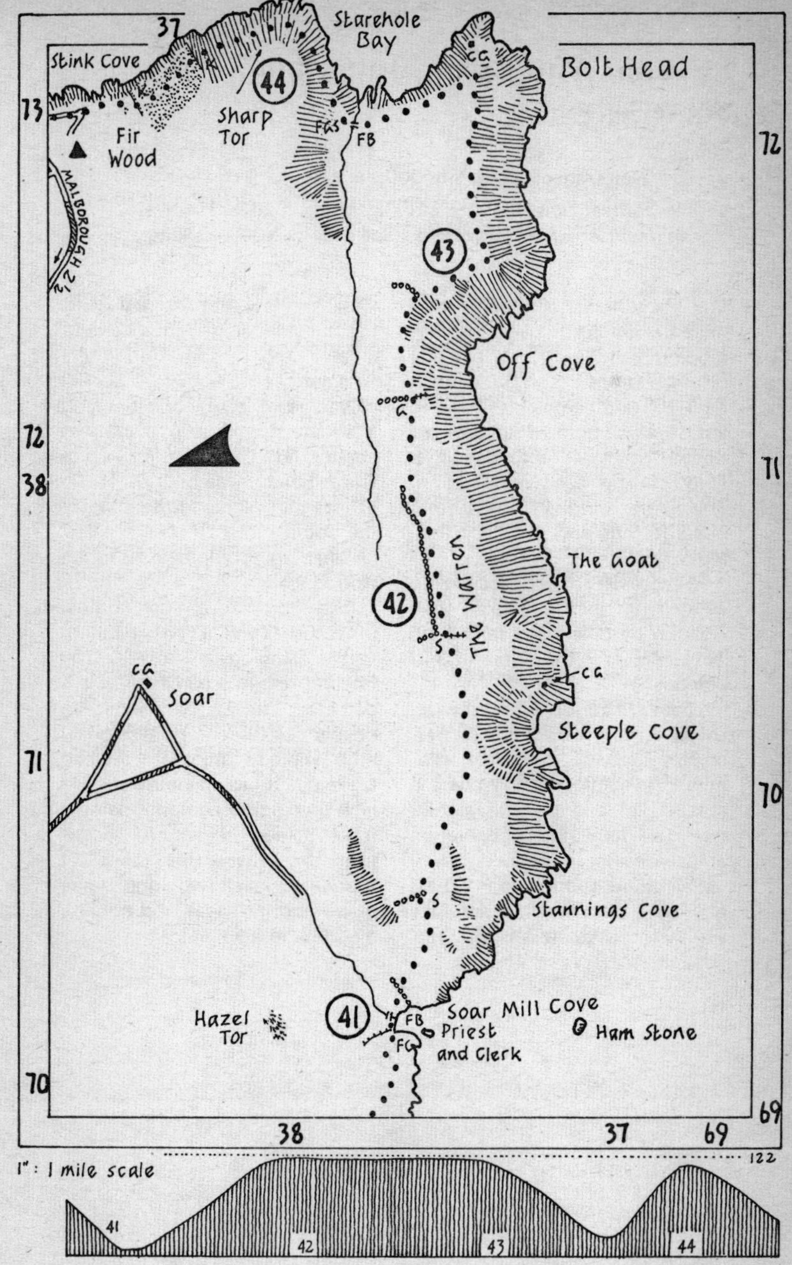

Stink Cove
Starehole Bay
Bolt Head
37
CG
73
Sharp Tor
Fir Wood
FnS
FB
72
MALBOROUGH
44
43
Off Cove
72
38
The Goat
The Warren
42
S
CG
CG
Soar
Steeple Cove
71
70
Stannings Cove
S
Hazel Tor
41
FB
Soar Mill Cove
Priest and Clerk
Ham Stone
FC
70
69
38
37
69
1": 1 mile scale
122
41
42
43
44

12. Splatcove Point, Salcombe, Bullock Cove

$4\frac{1}{2}$ miles
Maps: 1:25000 sheet SX73; 1:50000 sheet 202
Terrain: Pleasant easy walking into Salcombe, followed by a ferry crossing with splendid views and some easy, cliff-top walking.

Salcombe has shops, cafés, restaurants, public houses, accommodation, a Youth Hostel (just off the Path at South Sands near mile 45) and campsites. There is a bus garage from which services run to Plymouth and Kingsbridge. Early closing day is Thursdays. There are dinghies and other boats for hire and there is a sailing school.

In summer it is possible to avoid more than a mile of road walking by taking the ferry from South Sands to the centre of Salcombe.

There is a frequent ferry service, seven days a week, across Salcombe harbour to East Portlemouth. In summer, the last ferry is at 8.30 p.m. and in winter at 7.50 p.m. The ferry ceases operation an hour earlier in winter.

Salcombe (population 2,500) one of the most beautifully situated seaside towns in England, has few architectural gems but it is a most attractive harbour in a superb setting. During the summer the harbour will be full of yachts of all nationalities and a square-rigged ship may drop anchor. Fort Charles, the castle at North Sands, was built by Henry VIII as part of his fortification of the south coast. It was the last cavalier stronghold to yield to the Roundheads.

East Portlemouth has a post office stores and accommodation. Early closing day is Thursday. The fifteenth-century parish church is dedicated to St Winwaloe, an obscure sixth-century missionary who worked in both Brittany and Cornwall. It has an interesting old lych gate and a beautiful painted rood screen depicting scenes from the lives of the saints. St Winwaloe is shown in a white gown and red cloak and holding a church in his hand.

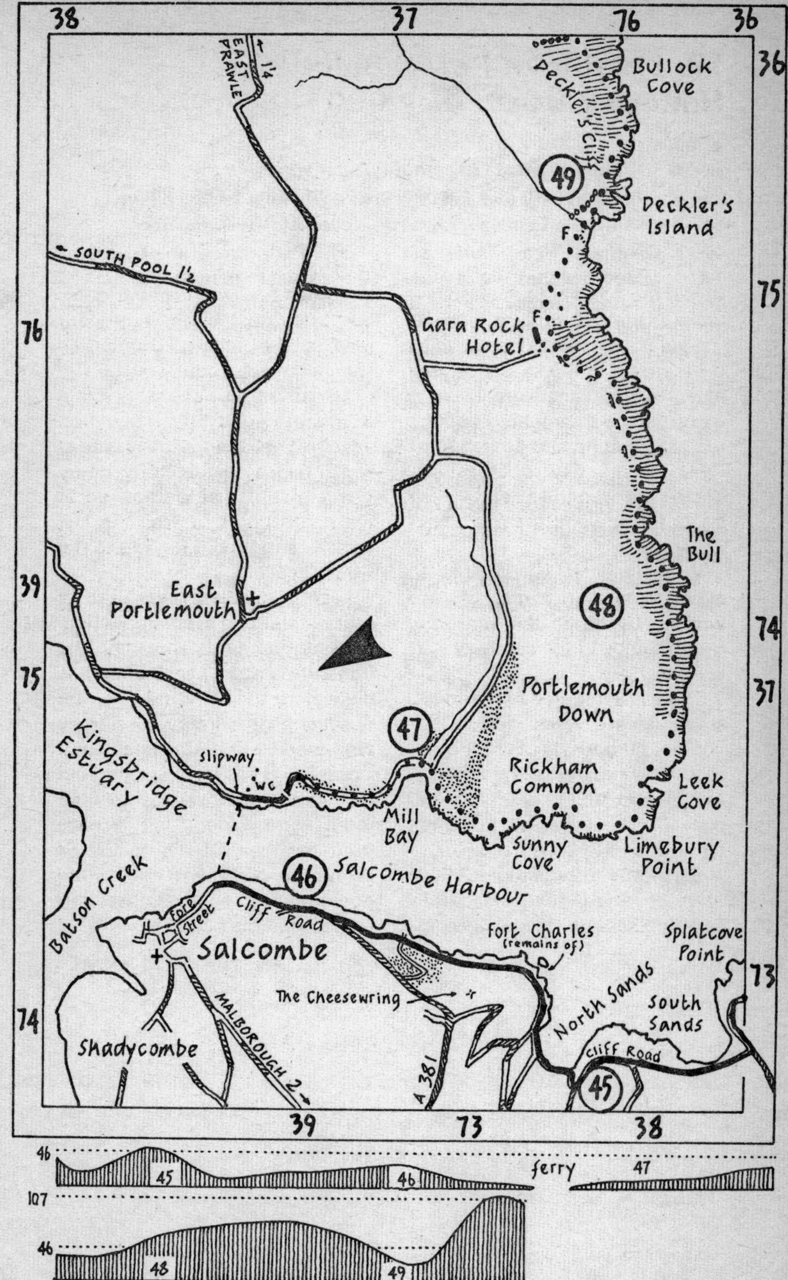
38
37
76
36
36
EAST PRAWLE
1¼
Deckler's Cliff
Bullock Cove
49
Deckler's Island
75
SOUTH POOL 1½
Gara Rock Hotel
F
F
76
The Bull
East Portlemouth
48
74
37
75
Portlemouth Down
47
Kingsbridge Estuary
slipway
wc
Rickham Common
Leek Cove
Mill Bay
Sunny Cove
Limebury Point
Batson Creek
46
Salcombe Harbour
Fore Street
Cliff Road
Fort Charles (remains of)
Splatcove Point
Salcombe
73
The Cheesewring
North Sands
South Sands
74
Shadycombe
MALBOROUGH 2
A 381
Cliff Road
45
39
73
38
46
45
46
ferry
47
107
46
48
49

13. Pig's Nose, Prawle Point, Horseley Cove, Stinking Cove

3 miles
Maps: 1:25000 sheet SX73; 1:50000 sheet 202
Terrain: More superb cliff-top walking with some steep hills.

Near Gammon Head there are two isolated beaches well below the footpath, Maceley Cove can be reached by a steep path.

East Prawle, a mile inland, has a pub, the Pig's Nose, which serves meals, and there is a bus service to Kingsbridge and East Portlemouth.

The Path takes the lower cliff (or in geologist's terms the 'raised beach') past the coastguard's cottages.

Walkers who venture on to the beach at Horseley Cove will find the curious sight of a bridleway sign pointing inland. This can only have been erected for the benefit of sea horses.

The Path runs at the bottom of the market garden through a series of gates and turns slightly inland opposite Ballsaddle Rock. A track leads off to a nice little beach at Lannacombe (map 14), with good bathing.

Prawle Point takes its name from the Old English word for lookout. It is the most southerly point in England outside Cornwall and is an excellent vantage point to watch bird migration. The whole area is good for butterflies, especially in sheltered places. Look out for small coppers, silver-studded blues and pearl-bordered fritillaries.

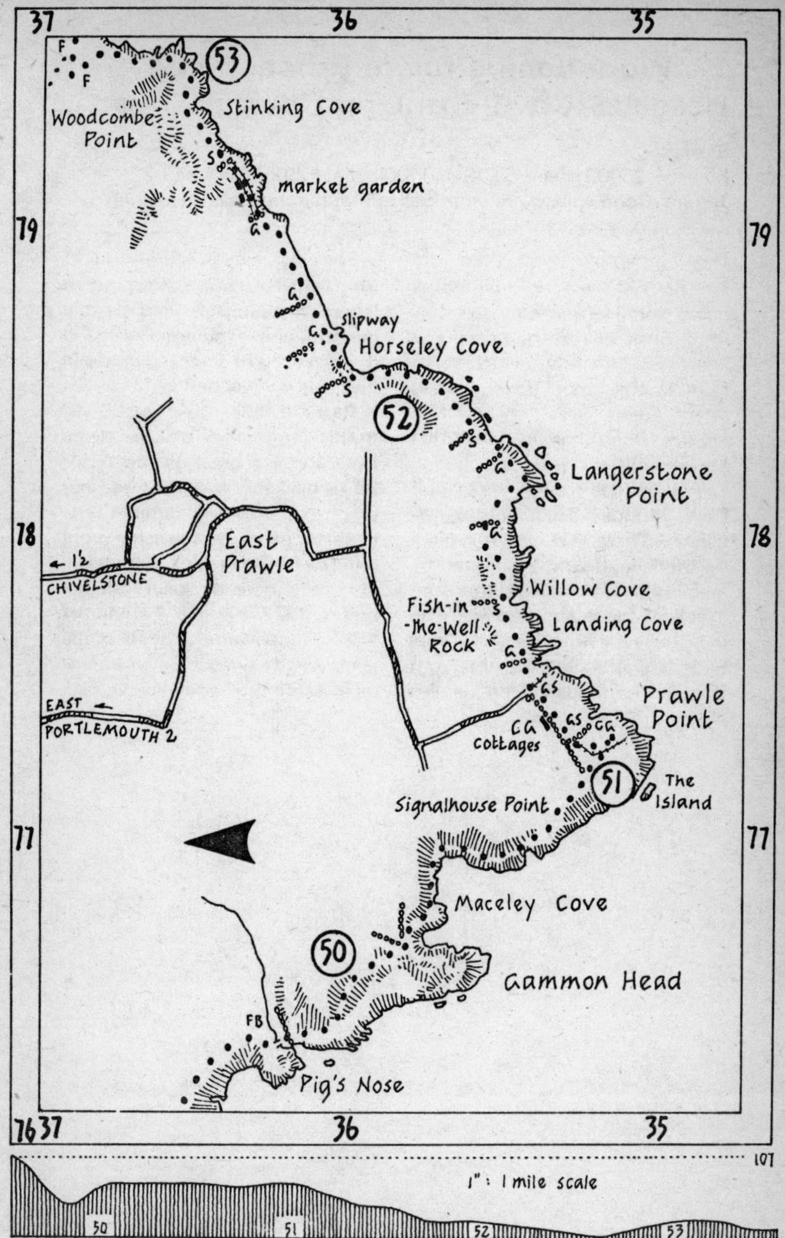

37
36
35
F
F
53
Stinking Cove
Woodcombe Point
market garden
S
79
79
G
G
G
slipway
Horseley Cove
S
52
S
Langerstone Point
G
G
78
78
East Prawle
Willow Cove
← 1½
CHIVELSTONE
Fish-in-the-Well Rock
S
Landing Cove
G
EAST
GS
Prawle Point
PORTLEMOUTH 2
CG
GS
CG
Cottages
51
The Island
Signalhouse Point
77
77
Maceley Cove
50
Gammon Head
FB
Pig's Nose
76 37
36
35
107
1": 1 mile scale
50
51
52
53

14. Woodcombe Sand, Lannacombe Beach, Start Point, Great Broad Cove

$3\frac{1}{2}$ miles
Maps: 1:25000 sheets SX73 and SX74/84; 1:50000 sheet 202
Terrain: Good walking as far as Start Point but then less interesting as the Path descends to Hallsands.

The Path is waymarked with blue paint from the car park to Hallsands. It keeps to the coast, but resist the temptation to swim from Mattiscombe Beach – it is dangerous!

Start Point has a fine lighthouse built in 1836 and still in use. It is open every afternoon from Monday to Saturday inclusive. There is a nature reserve on Start Point which is visited by many bird migrants, and this is an excellent place to observe them. It is believed that the nocturnal birds are attracted by the light from the lighthouse. 'Start' derives from the Anglo Saxon word 'steort', meaning 'tail', and the tidal currents and dangerous reefs off the point have wrecked many a fine ship.

Black Stone, just off Start Point, sank the *Marana* from Colombo in a great gale in 1891; 25 of her crew drowned and her cargo of sleepers littered the coast for miles. On the same night the *Dryad*, bound for Valparaiso, also sank near by losing all her crew of 22. On 28 September 1581, Henri Muge, a 'pirate of the sea', was hanged here in chains as a warning to other seafarers.

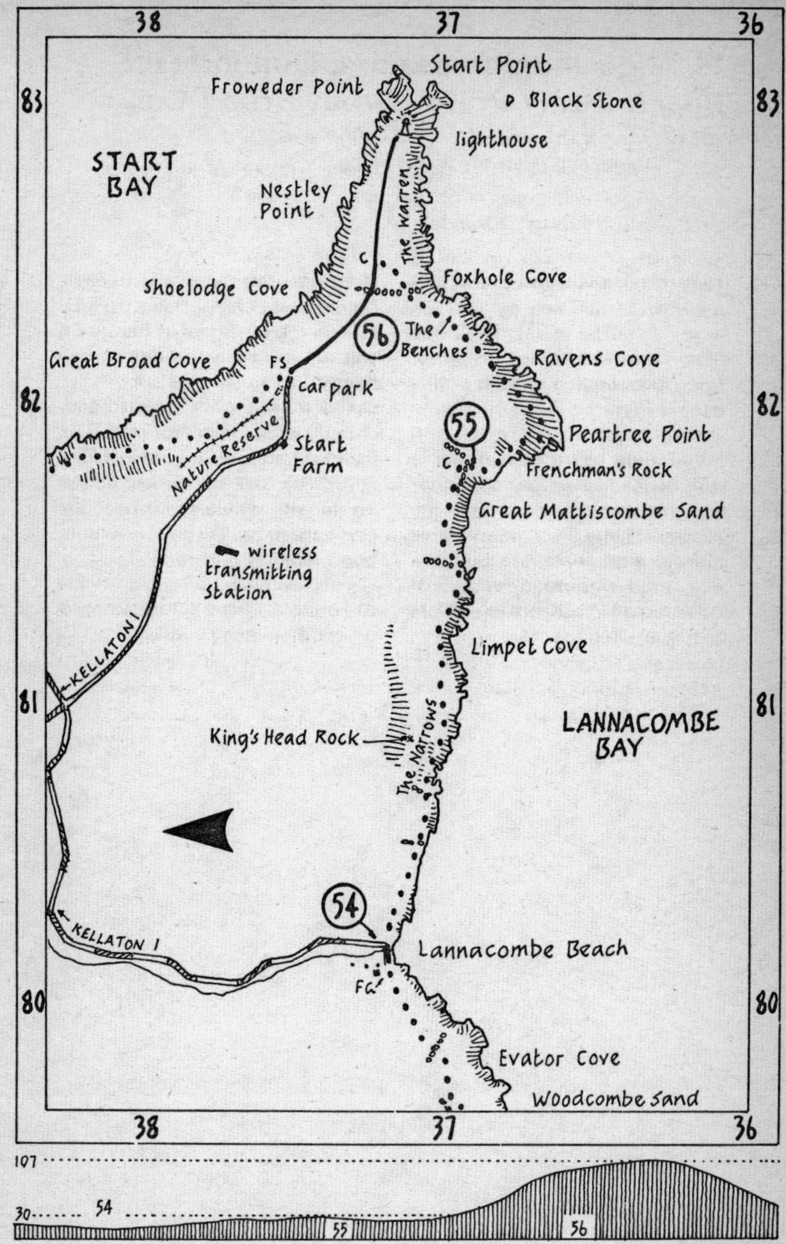

38
37
36
83
83
Start Point
Froweder Point
Black Stone
lighthouse
START BAY
Nestley Point
The Warren
C
Foxhole Cove
Shoelodge Cove
56
The Benches
Ravens Cove
Great Broad Cove
FS
car park
55
Peartree Point
82
82
Nature Reserve
Start Farm
C
Frenchman's Rock
Great Mattiscombe Sand
wireless transmitting station
KELLATON I
Limpet Cove
81
81
King's Head Rock
The Narrows
LANNACOMBE BAY
KELLATON I
54
Lannacombe Beach
FG
80
80
Evator Cove
Woodcombe Sand
38
37
36
107
30
54
55
56

15. Hallsands, Beesands, Dun Point

3 miles
Maps: 1:25000 sheet SX74/84; 1:50000 sheet 202
Terrain: Level, and relatively dull walking.

Hallsands has a post office. It used to be a village until it was engulfed by the sea in 1917. A large amount of shingle had been removed from the beach for making concrete dockyard extensions in Plymouth, weakening the sea defences.

Beesands has a post office, a pub, the Cricketers, accommodation, and on the north side of the village a large very unattractive caravan site. There is a bus service to Kingsbridge and East Portlemouth. There is a large slate quarry at Limpit rocks.

Both Hallsands and Beesands (formerly Hall Cellar and Beason Cellar) were once fishing villages and on the foreshore at Beesands can still be seen the rusting remains of winches and some salt-caked lobster pots. Three boats shot 80 pots, mostly for crab. The fishing tradition is now maintained by the numerous scuba divers with whom these beaches are very popular, and there is good bathing.

You can walk round Dun Point to Torcross village at low tide; the official Path climbs inland.

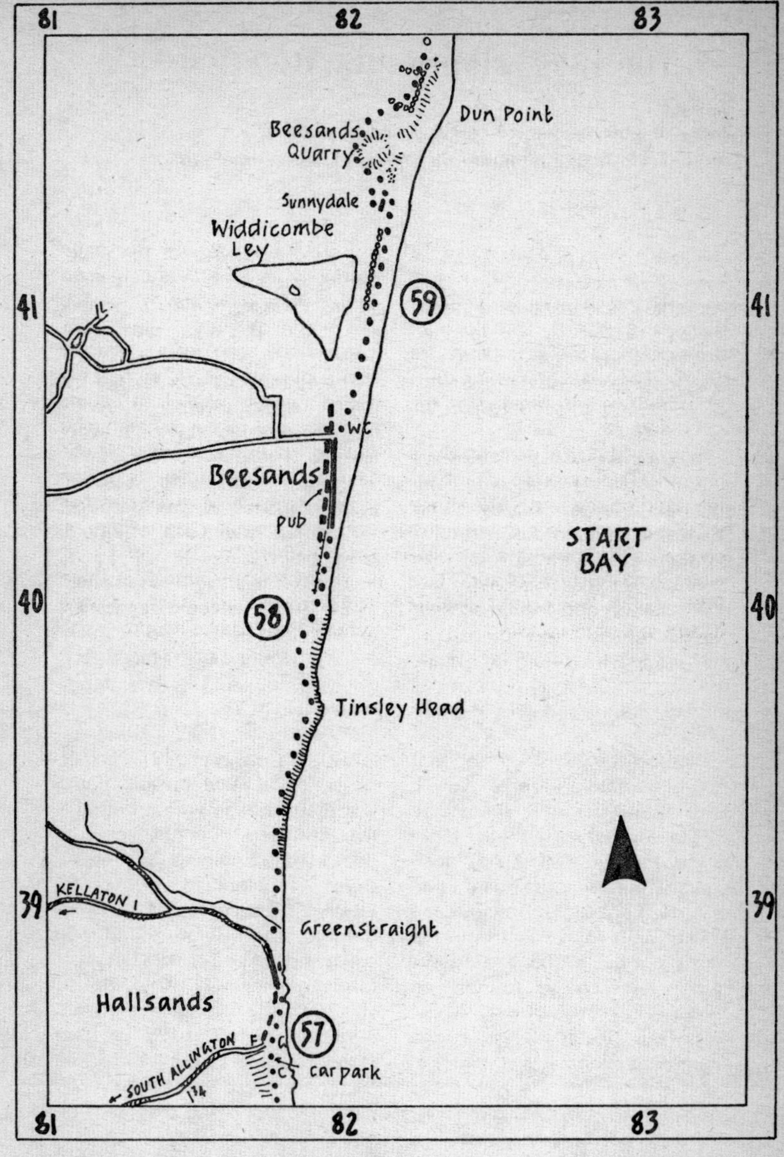

81
82
83
Dun Point
Beesands Quarry
Sunnydale
Widdicombe Ley
41
59
wc
Beesands
pub
START BAY
40
58
40
Tinsley Head
39
KELLATON
39
Greenstraight
Hallsands
57
SOUTH ALLINGTON
car park
81
82
83
46
57
58
59

16. Torcross, Slapton Sands

2½ miles
Maps: 1:25000 sheet SX74/84; 1:50000 sheet 202
Terrain: A dull section either on or very close to a main road.

Torcross has a grocer's shop, a post office, a café, a pub (the Start Bay) and accommodation. There is a bus service to Plymouth, Kingsbridge and Dartmouth. Early closing day is Saturday. There is a good beach for bathing.

At Torcross, walkers travelling east must decide whether to walk the next 6 miles, mostly along roads and in parts dull and dangerous, or catch the bus to Stoke Fleming. Torcross was once a pilchard station and fishermen kept Newfoundland dogs trained to swim out to returning boats through the surf, take the ropes in their mouths and carry them to shore.

Slapton Ley is an important 300-acre nature reserve with a Field Study Centre in the village of Slapton, which controls entry to the reserve. A path has been created between the main road and the Ley, which provides the walker with some relief from the heavy summer traffic. The reserve also includes two woods, difficult of access because of their steepness, but haunts of foxes and badgers. Legend has it that Excalibur, King Arthur's sword, lies hidden in the Ley. Boats for fishing pike, perch, rudd, roach and eels can be hired from the Field Centre. Birds to be seen include cranes, marsh harriers, spotted crakes and the great reed warblers.

The monument was erected by the United States army to record their thanks to local people, who had to evacuate their homes when the sands were used for training assault troops destined for Normandy in 1944. It would have been more fitting for a monument to have been erected by the British to record our thanks for American help, without which the war would have taken a very different course. The evacuation is recorded in *The Land Changed its Face* by Grace Bradbeer (David & Charles, 1973).

Slapton, ¾ mile off the Path, is a pretty village with an attractive fourteenth-century church dedicated to St James. Sir Guy de Bryan, a standard bearer to Edward III and one of the first Knights of the Garter, founded a collegiate chantry here in the fourteenth century. One tower still survives, and there are also remnants of the walls in the Priory, a late-Georgian house. Slapton is noted for its sub-tropical horticulture, and oranges and figs grow profusely.

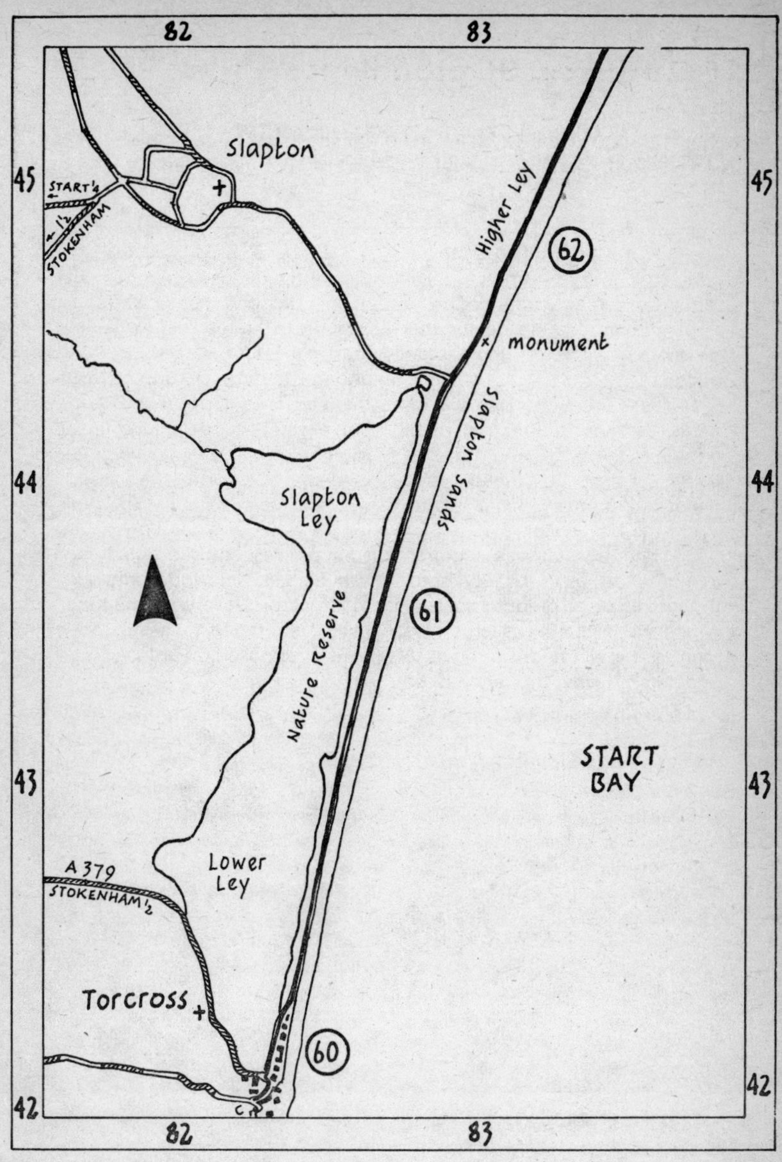

82
83
Slapton
45
START¼
STOKENHAM 1½
Higher Ley
62
monument
Slapton Sands
44
Slapton Ley
61
Nature Reserve
START BAY
43
A 379
STOKENHAM ½
Lower Ley
Torcross
60
42
82
83
15 60 61 62

17. Strete Gate, Strete, Blackpool Sands

3 miles
Maps: 1:25000 sheet SX74/84; 1:50000 sheet 202
Terrain: This section is entirely along roads.

Strete has a post office stores, a pub (the King's Arms) which serves meals, accommodation, a Youth Hostel, a campsite and bus services to Plymouth and Kingsbridge.

This is a dull section entirely on roads, as there is no Coast Path. Between miles 64 and 65 it is better to take the minor road rather than the official route along the busy main road.

Blackpool Sands has acquired a reputation as a beauty spot, though, after the glorious scenery which the walker has seen on his journey, he will find it difficult to understand why this should be so. Perhaps it is because the pine-fringed beach lies near the main road and has a large car park. In 1404, the Bretons landed from a fleet of 300 ships in an attempt to take Dartmouth from the rear. They were defeated at a battle which was described as 'the scomfiture of Blackpolle'. The women of Dartmouth distinguished themselves by 'the hurling of flints and of pipples and such artillery and did greatly advance their husbands' and kinfolks' victory'. Warwick the Kingmaker is reputed to have landed here to oppose Edward IV.

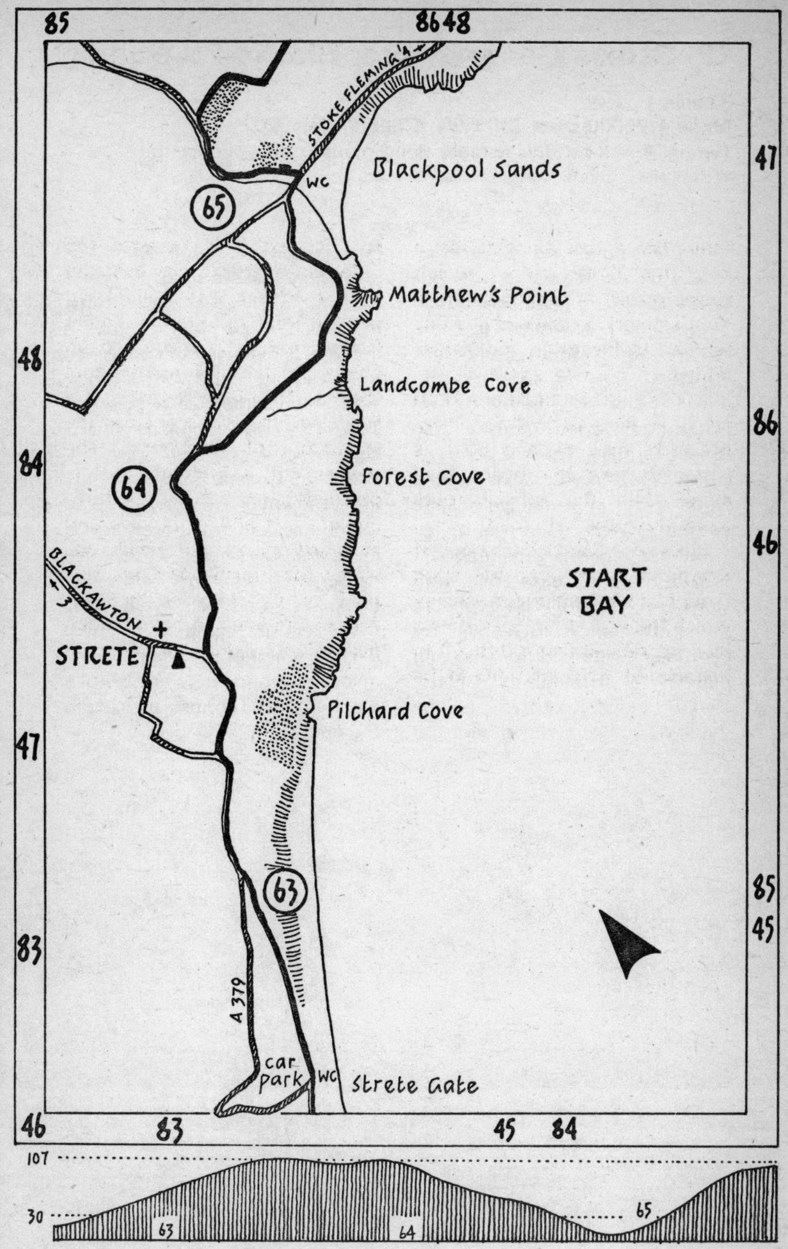

85
8648
STOKE FLEMING '4
Blackpool Sands
WC
65
Matthew's Point
48
Landcombe Cove
84
Forest Cove
64
BLACKAWTON
3
STRETE
START
BAY
Pilchard Cove
47
63
A 379
83
car
park WC Strete Gate
46
83
45
84
47
86
46
85
45
107
30
63
64
65

18. Stoke Fleming, Blackstone Point

3½ miles
Maps: 1:25000 sheet SX85/95; 1:50000 sheet 202
Terrain: About half the distance is still upon roads, but once the coast is regained there is some pleasant walking.

Stoke Fleming has a grocer's shop, a café, a post office, accommodation, a campsite, public houses and bus services to Dartmouth and Plymouth. Early closing days vary from shop to shop and it should be possible to find at least one open on every day except Sunday. There is a campsite at Leonard's Cove. Stoke Fleming is an attractive village with a church, dedicated to St Peter, containing a very fine fourteenth-century brass of John Corp and his wife. The imposing thirteenth-century tower was for centuries a landmark for shipping making for Dartmouth. George Barker Bidder, known as the 'human calculator', lived here and later became George Stephenson's principal assistant. He could do enormously complicated sums in his head.

From Stoke Fleming take the right turn at Windward Corner. After ¾ mile there is a National Trust car park. Opposite this a signpost directs you back towards the Coastal Path, descending towards Compass Cove, which has a shingle beach and is good for swimming. There is a detour at Blackstone Point over the stile to a bridge over the sea.

Walkers travelling west must decide whether to walk the 6 miles of road between Stoke Fleming and Torcross or to take the bus.

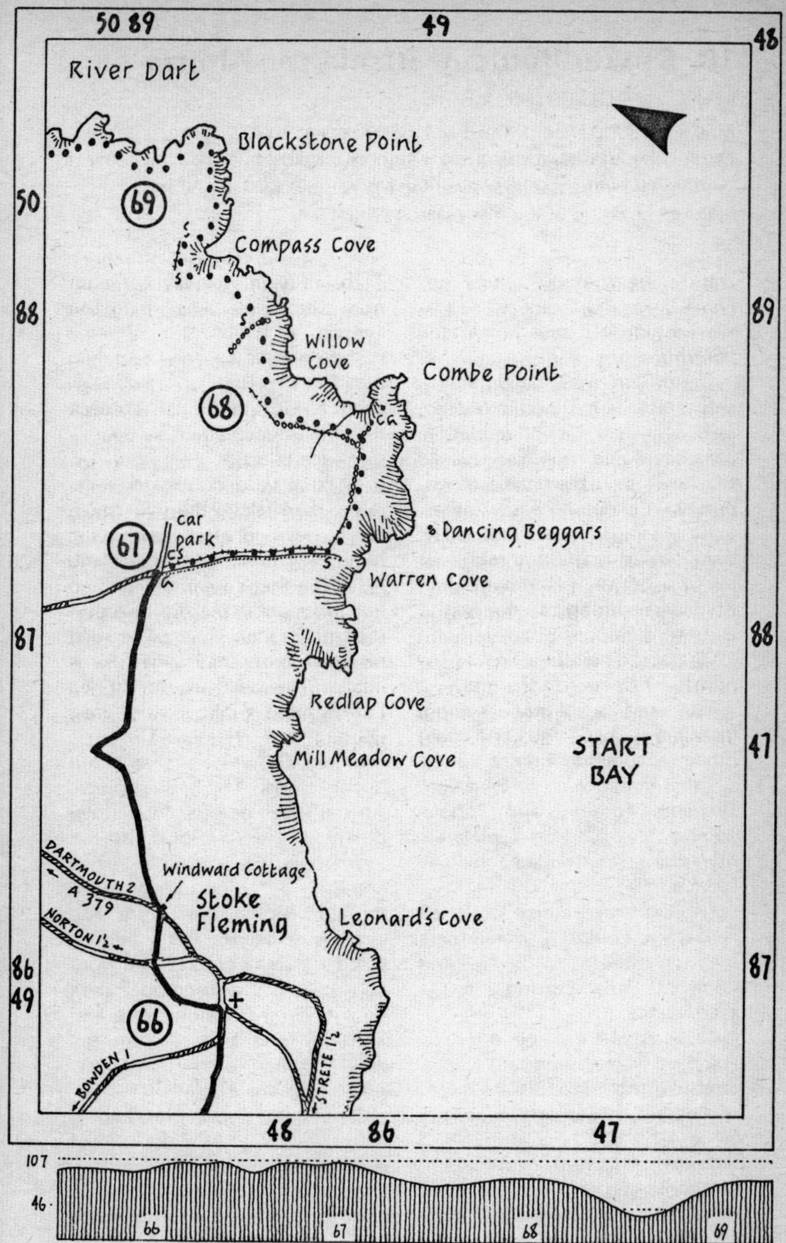

50 89
49
48
River Dart
Blackstone Point
69
Compass Cove
88
Willow Cove
Combe Point
68
89
car park
67
Dancing Beggars
Warren Cove
87
88
Redlap Cove
Mill Meadow Cove
START BAY
47
DARTMOUTH 2
A 379
Windward Cottage
Stoke Fleming
Leonard's Cove
NORTON 1½
86
49
86
87
66
BOWDEN 1
STRETE 1½
48
86
47
107
46
66
67
68
69

19. Castle Point, Dartmouth, Kingswear, Scabbacombe Lane

5½ miles
Maps: 1:25000 sheet SX85/95; 1:50000 sheet 202
Terrain: The route lies entirely along roads but is relieved by the pleasant crossing of the River Dart by the ferry.

During the summer a ferry operates from the Castle to Kingswear which will save some road walking.

Dartmouth has food shops, cafés, restaurants, public houses, a post office, accommodation, campsites and bus services to Blackawton, Townstall, Kingsbridge, Plymouth and Totnes. Early closing day is Wednesday. Two ferries operate throughout the year between Dartmouth and Kingswear during the hours of 7 a.m. (8 a.m. on Sundays) and 10.50 p.m. There is a Tourist Information Centre on the quay.

Kingswear has a grocer's shop, cafés, a public house, a post office, accommodation, a campsite and bus services to Paignton, Brixham, Torquay and Babbacombe. There is also a privately owned steam-hauled railway service, the Torbay Steam Railway Company, which operates services to Paignton, where there are connections to Exeter and London. Early closing day is Wednesday.

At Kingswear, east-bound walkers have some important decisions to make. The 38 miles between Kingswear and Starcross (mile 109) are largely dull and urbanized, much of it over roads, with only one or two stretches of good walking (see p. 9). A case can be made for taking the Torbay Steam Railway (or bus) from Kingswear to Paignton (which runs in the summer months and Easter only) and then by British Rail to Starcross (before booking the ticket, check that the Starcross ferry is operating – see p. 86).

Walkers who decide to walk, rather than taking the train, must cross the road after leaving the ferry, pass under the arch, climb up Alma Steps near the church and turn right to pick up the coast road at Beacon Road. The road becomes a footpath, then turns inland. The next section of the Path is not a public right of way, although the National Trust has acquired Brownstone Farm and hopes to open it up in due course. At the fork bear right slightly downhill and turn right over a footbridge just before a white cottage. A rock path goes through Brownstone Farm and along a tarmac road to a T-junction by a small copse. Turn right and follow Scabbacombe Lane until it becomes a stony track and ends at Man Sands. Note the lime kiln and a row of coastguard cottages.

Dartmouth Castle was largely rebuilt in 1481 and is the earliest surviving castle specifically designed for ordnance. There is another castle on the opposite bank and between them they

continued on p. 64

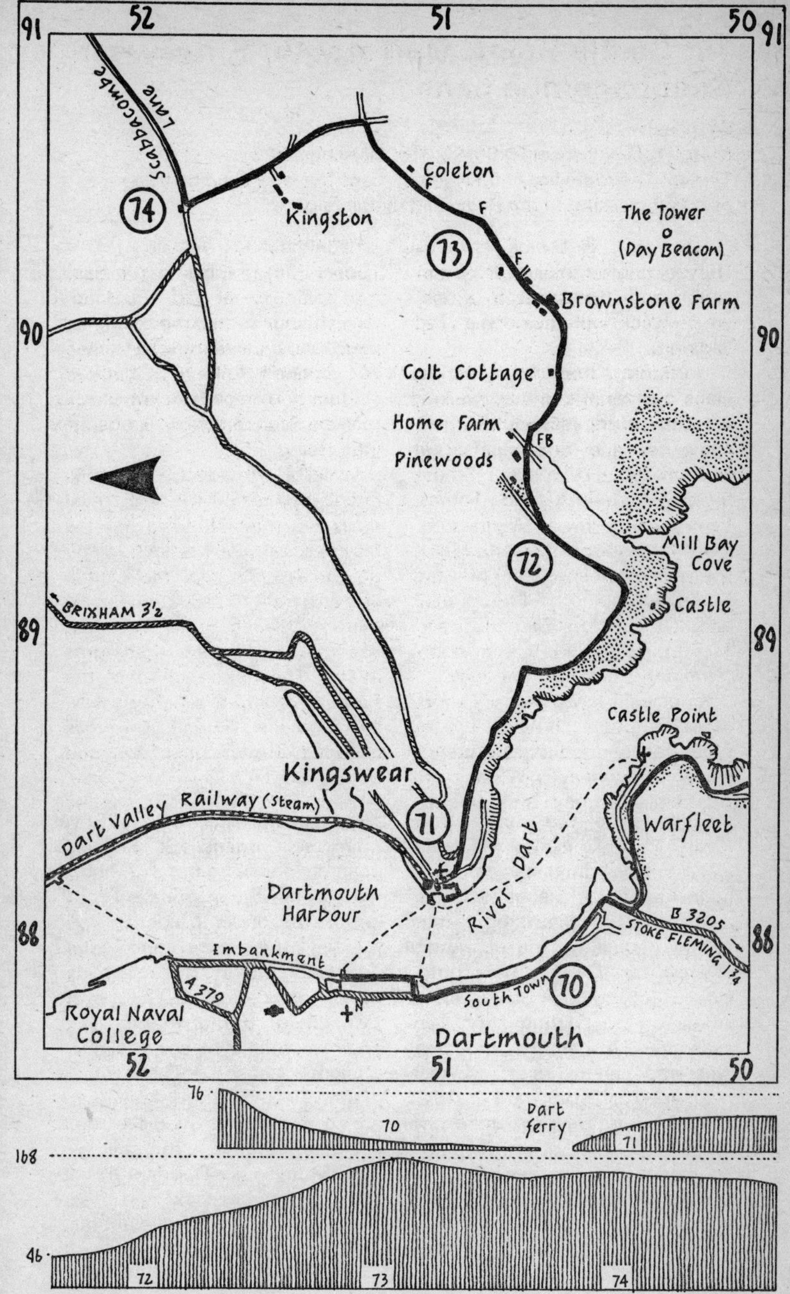

91
52
51
50
91
Scabbacombe Lane
74
Coleton
F
Kingston
F
73
F
The Tower
o
(Day Beacon)
Brownstone Farm
90
Colt Cottage
Home Farm
FB
Pinewoods
Mill Bay
Cove
72
Castle
BRIXHAM 3½
89
Castle Point
Kingswear
Warfleet
Dart Valley Railway (steam)
71
River Dart
88
Dartmouth
Harbour
B 3205
STOKE FLEMING 1¾
Embankment
A 379
70
South Town
Royal Naval
College
N
Dartmouth
52
51
50
76
Dart
ferry
70
71
168
46
72
73
74

20. Woodhuish, Man Sands

2½ miles
Maps: 1:25000 sheet SX85/95; 1:50000 sheet 202
Terrain: Dull walking along quiet country lanes.

Man Sands is a most attractive beauty spot and eastward-bound walkers will be pleased to reach it to pick up the Coast Path again.

Westward-bound walkers now face 5 miles of dull road walking, as the Countryside Commission have so far been unable to persuade the landowners to permit a Coast Path to cross their land.

The stretch of path south from Man Sands past Long Sands and Scabbacombe Sands is likely to be opened following a public inquiry. The path is open between Scabbacombe Sands and the Head.

continued from p. 62

could control the movement of warships on the river. By Henry VIII's time, guns had improved considerably in range and efficiency so that the harbour could be protected by the cannon of Dartmouth Castle. The Butterwalk, an attractive row of shops and offices dating from the seventeenth century, has been restored after being severely damaged in an air raid in 1943. Near by is Newcomen House, where one of Thomas Newcomen's steam engines, built in 1725, can be seen working. There are two memorials to Thomas Newcomen in the beautiful Royal Avenue Gardens. St Saviour's church dates from 1372 and is famous for the magnificent south door, the fifteenth-century rood screen, the carved and gilded stone pulpit and the Jacobean west gallery. It is well worth wandering round the maze of narrow streets to see the many quaint houses. The Pilgrim Fathers' ship, the *Mayflower*, anchored off the medieval quay of Bayard's Cove before sailing to Massachusetts. Dartmouth harbour, dominated by the Royal Naval College, is very beautiful.

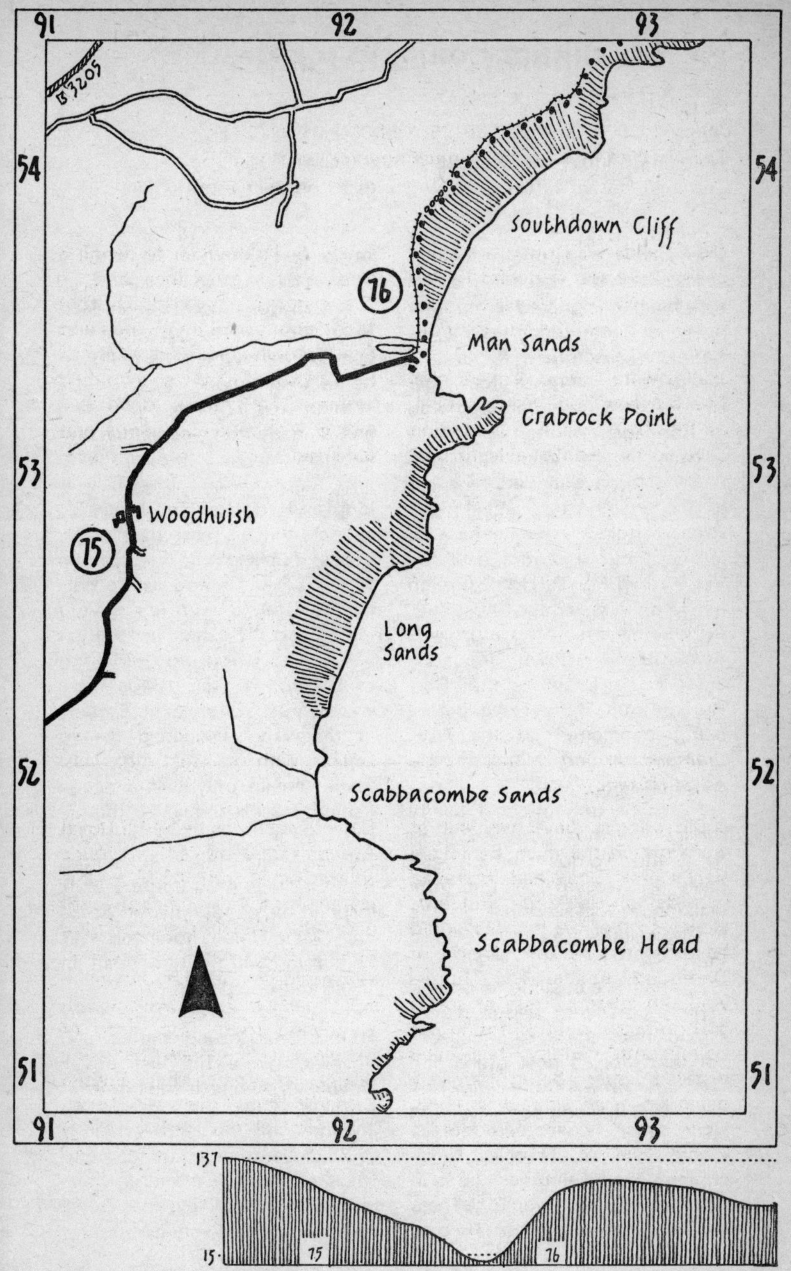

B 3205
Southdown Cliff
Man Sands
Crabrock Point
Woodhuish
Long
Sands
Scabbacombe Sands
Scabbacombe Head
75
76
137
15
75
76

21. Sharkham Point, Berry Head, Brixham

4 miles
Maps: 1:25000 sheet SX85/95; 1:50000 sheet 202
Terrain: Pleasant cliff-top walking until the descent into Brixham.

Berry Head, a popular beauty spot, is a maze of footpaths and has been designated a country park. The promontory has a lighthouse, a coastguard lookout, a navigation marker, a fort built during the Napoleonic wars and an Iron Age hill fort.

Titus and Vespasian are reputed to have landed here and it is certainly true that many Roman artefacts have been found at Ash Hole, a cavern near the Berry Head House Hotel (which used to be a military hospital). Napoleon waited on board H M S *Bellerophon* (known affectionately to her crew as the 'Billy Ruffian') off Berry Head before being transferred to the *Northumberland* and sailing to exile on St Helena.

From May to September, a ferry service operates between Brixham and Torquay which can make a pleasant change from walking, as this section is not the most attractive part of the Coast Path.

Brixham is a bustling resort and fishing port with shops, cafés, public houses, restaurants, accommodation, a post office and bus services to Kingswear, Torquay, Babbacombe, Newton Abbot and Sharkham Point. Early closing day is Wednesday.

A bus goes from Berry Head Road around the town to Fishcombe Road, where the path can be rejoined.

Brixham is a Saxon royal estate and an early Iron Age settlement. Brixham Cavern, in Mount Pleasant Road, is more than 600 ft long and contains the bones of extinct animals and much evidence of palaeolithic man. On the Harbour Pier is an obelisk to William of Orange, who first landed in England at Brixham in 1688 on his way to being crowned King of England. In the 1840s there were almost 300 ships here, many of them the distinctive fishing smack with its rust-red sails. There remain only half a dozen fishing vessels today, all motorized. Henry Lyte was vicar of Brixham and the sun setting while he was on a country walk inspired his popular hymn 'Abide with Me'. Flora Thompson was here from 1940 until her death in 1947 and completed *Still Glides the Stream* during that time. Francis Brett Young, the popular novelist, wrote his first novel, *Deep Sea*, while living in Brixham.

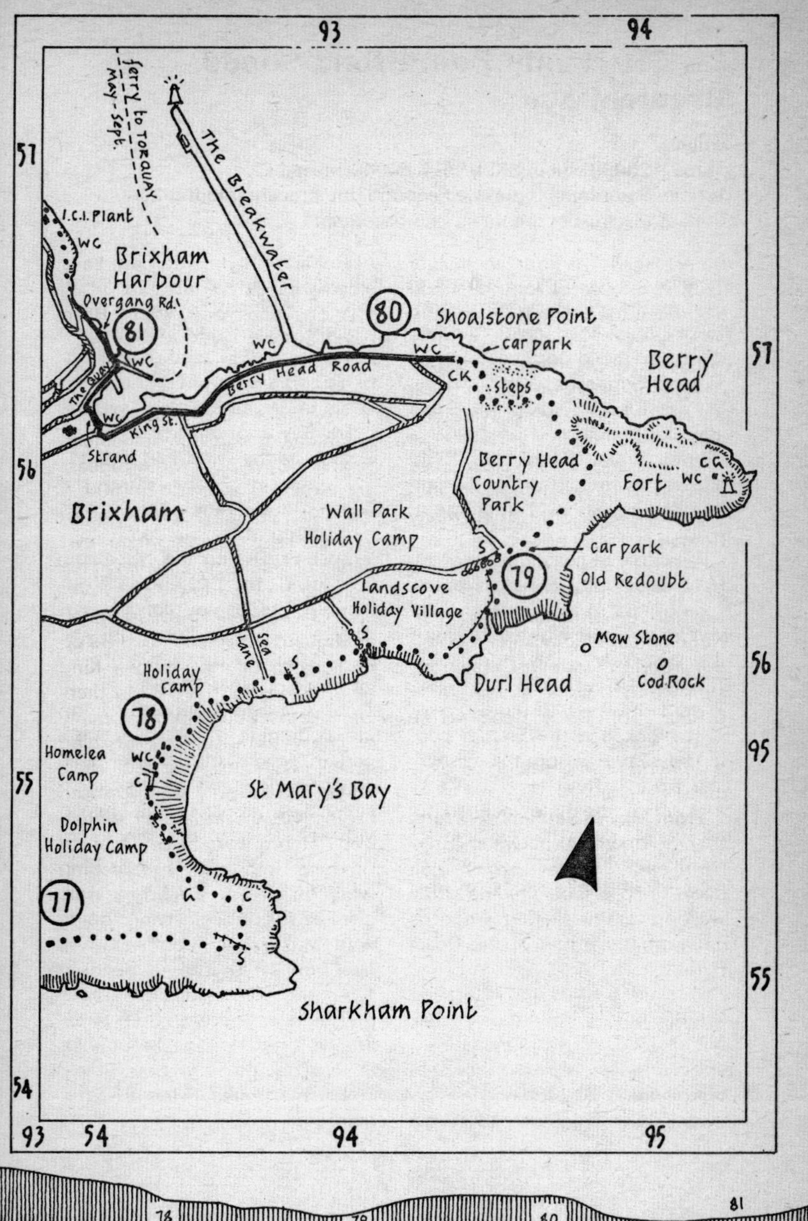

93
94
57
ferry to TORQUAY May-Sept.
The Breakwater
I.C.I. Plant
WC
Brixham Harbour
Overgang Rd.
81
WC
80
Shoalstone Point
car park
Berry Head
57
WC
CK
steps
Berry Head Road
The Quay
WC
King St.
56
WC
Strand
Brixham
Wall Park Holiday Camp
Berry Head Country Park
Fort
WC
CG
Landscove Holiday Village
S
79
car park
Old Redoubb
Sea Lane
S
S
Durl Head
Mew Stone
Cod Rock
56
Holiday Camp
S
95
78
WC
C
Homelea Camp
St Mary's Bay
55
Dolphin Holiday Camp
77
C
C
S
55
Sharkham Point
54
93
54
94
95
78
79
80
81

22. Churston Cove, Broad Sands, Saltern Cove

4 miles
Maps: 1:25000 sheet SX85/95; 1:50000 sheet 202
Terrain: This stretch is pleasant enough but not very exciting.
One is conscious of the threat of urban sprawl.

The area around mile 82 is a maze of footpaths, and eastward-bound walkers must keep inside the belt of trees to avoid going astray.

Broad Sands has bus services to Paignton, Babbacombe, Torquay, Kingswear and Brixham.

From Broad Sands the Path follows the line of the Dart Steam Railway as far as Goodrington Sands.

The curve of coastline between Berry Head (map 21) and Hope's Nose (map 25) is called Tor Bay, which until the eighteenth century was very thinly populated. During the Seven Years War, Sir Edward Hawke with the Channel Fleet blockaded the French port of Brest, preventing the French fleet from putting to sea. Naval thinking at the time inclined to the belief that the blockading season had to end in September because of the severity of the autumn gales, but Hawke hung on until November, when a particularly violent gale forced him off his station. Instead of making for harbour he sought refuge from the storm in the sheltered waters of Tor Bay and returned to Brest as soon as the wind had abated. This was in 1759, when he defeated the French by superb seamanship at the Battle of Quiberon Bay. During the Napoleonic wars the Channel fleet adopted the same tactics. The officers of the fleet quickly learned that Tor Bay was a pleasant place to live as well as to shelter from the storms and from this beginning grew the huge modern resort of Torbay. The rapid development of the area received a considerable boost with the arrival of the railway in 1848. Until this time Torquay was but a village.

58
89
59
Goodrington
A 3022 KINGSKERSWELL
PAIGNTON 1½
85
Sugar Loaf Hill
Saltern Cove
A 379
Armchair Rock
Dart Valley Railway
Shell Cove
84
Broad Sands
car park
wc
GS
Churston Point
S
83
Elbury Cove
Churston Ferrers
Golf Course
82
The Grove
G
Fishcombe Point
FC
Torbay Holiday Chalets
Churston Cove
BRIXHAM 1½
steps
wc
Holiday Camp
I C I Marine Research Station
car park
57
59
90
89
91
90
56
58
92
91
56
92
57

46
82
83
84
85

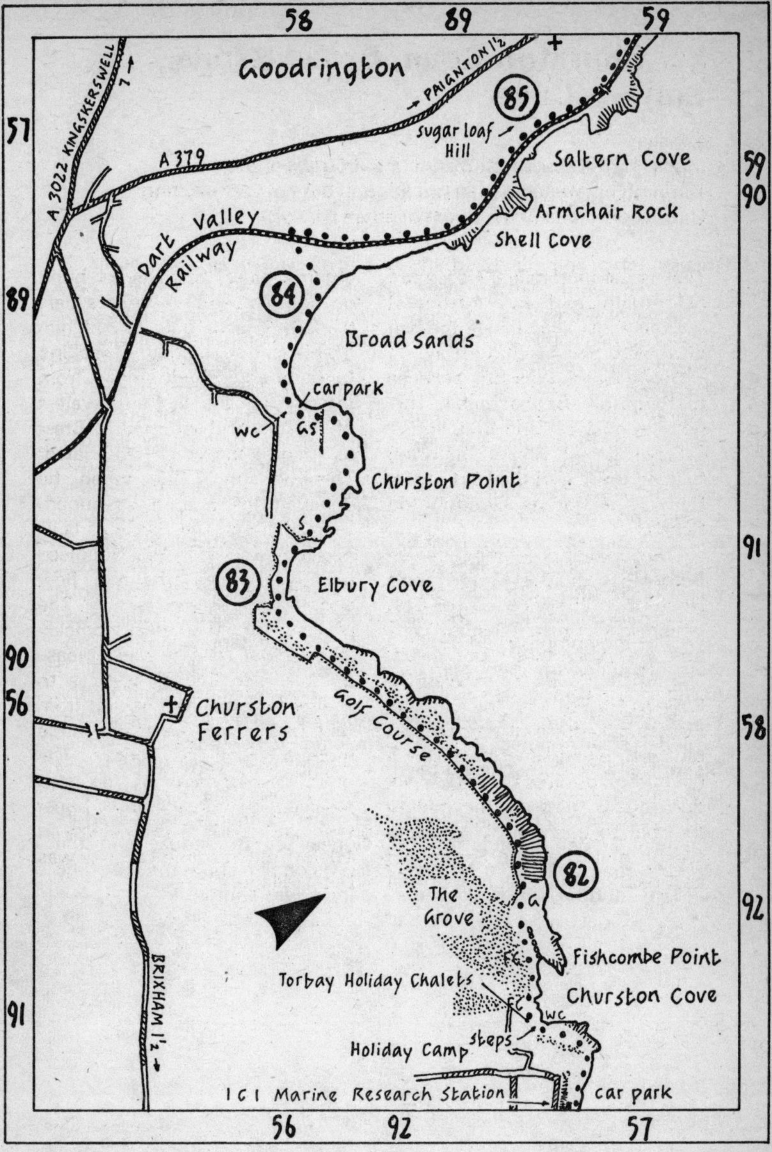

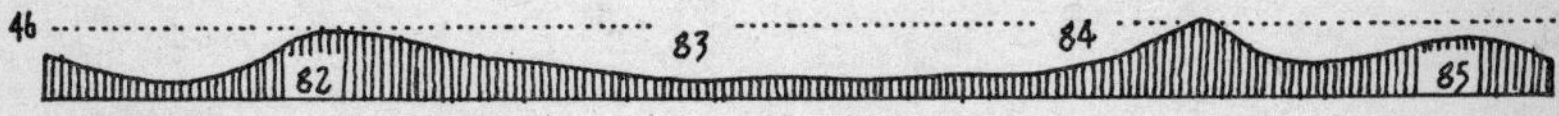

23. Goodrington Sands, Fairy Cove, Paignton

3 miles
Maps: 1:25000 sheet SX85/95; 1:50000 sheet 202
Terrain: Dull road walking all the way.

This stretch is completely urbanized and not worth walking. Walkers travelling east are strongly advised to catch the bus to Babbacombe and resume their walk from there.

Goodrington Sands has bus services to Paignton, Torquay, Brixham, Babbacombe, Kingswear and Newton Abbot.

Paignton has shops, public houses, cafés, restaurants, banks, a post office, accommodation, a bus service with both local and long-distance services to all points of the compass and a railway station with services to Exeter and London as well as to Kingswear on the privately owned steam-hauled Torbay Steam Railway. Early closing day is Wednesday.

The Paignton Zoological and Botanical Garden extends for 75 acres, is open daily from 10 a.m. to 7 p.m., and has a good collection of rare trees and shrubs. A sub-tropical house heated only by the sun is divided into geographical components and birds fly freely inside the house. St John, the parish church of Paignton, is mainly fifteenth-century, but was built on the site of a Saxon church and has some evidence of the old Norman church. There is a splendid Norman west door, an eleventh-century font, a skeleton monument and a dog door in the north doorway. Probably the best feature is the magnificent Kirkham Chantry. Connoisseurs of the bizarre should visit Oldway House, built by the American Singer family of sewing machine fame. It much resembles the kind of mansion to be found in the fashionable resorts of New England. Singer brought Isadora Duncan to the house and the television film about the life of the dancer was shot here.

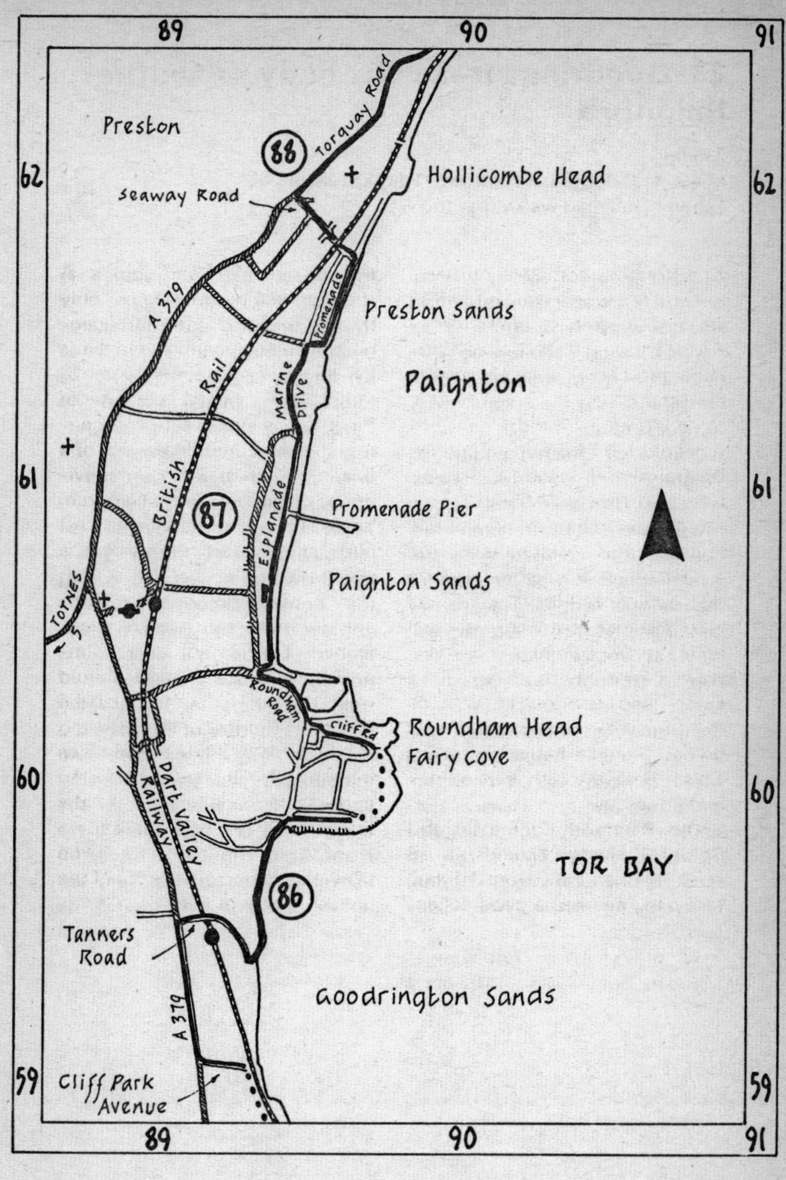

89
90
91
62
Preston
88
Torquay Road
Hollicombe Head
seaway Road
Preston Sands
Paignton
61
A 379
British Rail
Promenade
Marine Drive
87
Esplanade
Promenade Pier
Paignton Sands
Totnes
Roundham Road
Cliff Rd
Roundham Head
Fairy Cove
60
Dart Valley Railway
TOR BAY
86
Tanners Road
Goodrington Sands
A 379
59
Cliff Park Avenue
89
90
91
15
86
87
88

24. Livermead Head, Torquay, Meadfoot Sea Road

$3\frac{1}{2}$ miles
Maps: 1:25000 sheet SX86/96; 1:50000 sheet 202
Terrain: Dull urban walking.

Another section of the Path which is completely urbanized and not worth walking.

West-bound walkers who want a change from walking should consider taking the summer ferry to Brixham.

Torbay, of which Torquay and Paignton form constituent parts, is, after Plymouth, the largest town on the Path. In summer its beaches are crowded with sun worshippers who gather here for their annual festival. The scantily clad disciples of the sun god will stare at you strangely as you march through wearing thick socks, boots and breeches.

Torquay has shops, cafés, restaurants, public houses, banks, a post office, accommodation, campsites and an extensive network of bus and long-distance coach services. Trains run to Paignton, Exeter and London. Early closing days are Wednesday and Saturday.

Torquay's Torre Abbey was founded originally in 1196 as a Praemonstratensian monastery but was made into a home after the Reformation. It is now owned by the municipality and is used as an art gallery. During the middle years of the last century Torquay became a popular resort, especially among writers, and was described as 'the queen of watering places'. Tennyson thought it to be 'the loveliest sea village in England'. Elizabeth Barrett Browning stayed here during her convalescence at Beacon Terrace, now the Regina Hotel; Bulwer Lytton, the best-selling novelist of the nineteenth century, died here in 1873; Eden Phillpotts, author of the play *The Farmer's Wife*, lived here and encouraged the young Agatha Christie, who was born in the town; Sean O'Casey made it his home from 1955 until his death in 1964; and Charles Kingsley, author of *Westward Ho!* and *The Water Babies*, stayed for a time at Livermead Cottage.

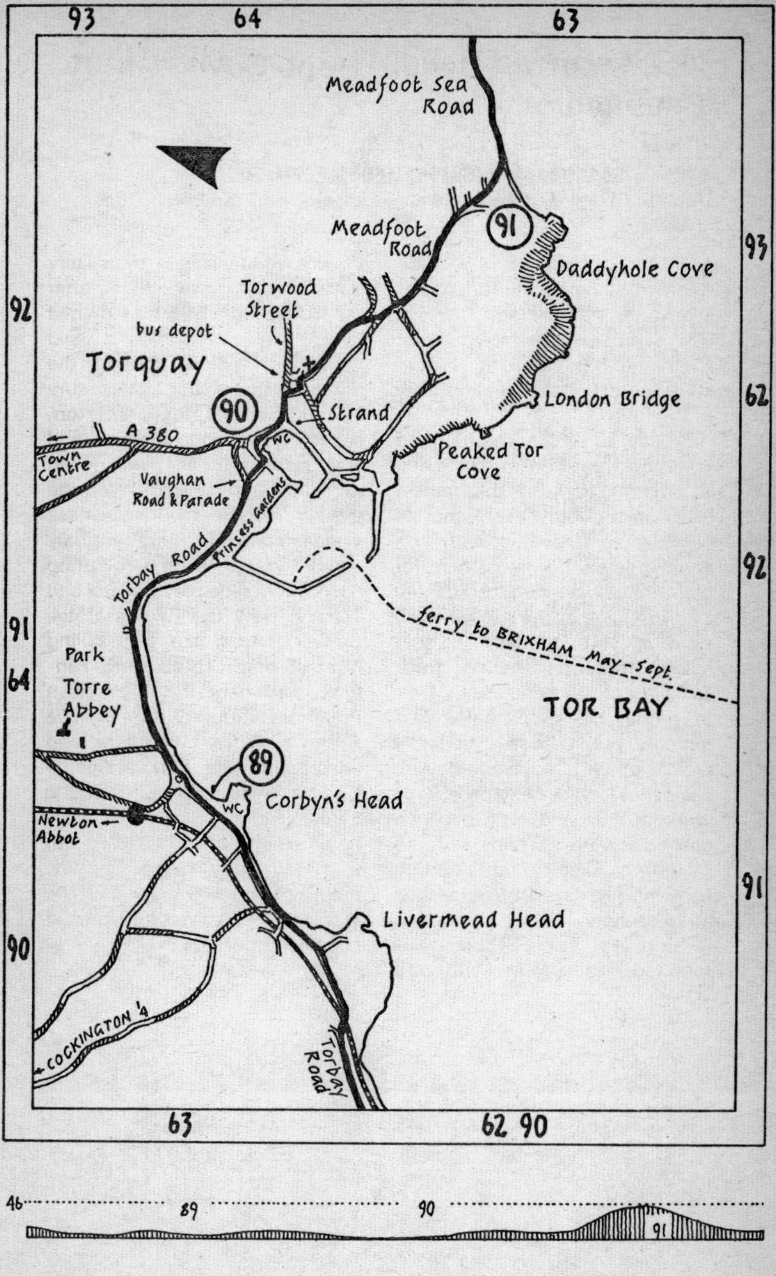

93
64
63
Meadfoot Sea Road
Meadfoot Road
91
Daddyhole Cove
93
Torwood Street
bus depot
Torquay
92
London Bridge
62
90
Strand
Peaked Tor Cove
A 380
Town Centre
WC
Vaughan Road & Parade
Princess Gardens
92
Torbay Road
ferry to BRIXHAM May - Sept.
91
64
Park
Torre Abbey
TOR BAY
89
WC
Corbyn's Head
Newton Abbot
91
Livermead Head
90
COCKINGTON
Torbay Road
63
62 90
46
89
90
91

25. Meadfoot Beach, Hope Cove, Babbacombe

3 miles
Maps: 1:25000 sheet SX86/96; 1:50000 sheet 202
Terrain: Easy walking along well-used paths popular with holiday-makers.

East-bound walkers will be relieved to leave the roads behind and resume walking along the Coast Path at Brandy Cove.

Kent's Cavern in Wellswood (which can be reached by keeping to the road after Hope Cove, rather than turning on to the coastal path) is a series of connecting limestone caves with much evidence of palaeolithic occupation (material ranges from 100,000 to 8000 B C) and has been described as the oldest house in Britain. A wide range of flint implements, bone tools and the bones of extinct animals such as the woolly rhinoceros, the mammoth and the cave lion have been found and are to be seen in the Torquay Natural History Museum in Babbacombe Road (open from 10 a.m. to 5 p.m. on weekdays). There are strikingly large and beautiful stalactites and stalagmites.

Hope's Nose has the largest kittiwake colony in Devon (about 150 pairs) and is much used by migratory birds, including the purple sandpiper.

Babbacombe Model Village occupies a four-acre site in a combe running down to the sea. 800 varieties of trees and shrubs have been planted, including a notable collection of dwarf conifers. It is open from Easter to October daily from 9 a.m. to 10 p.m., and from November to Easter from 9 a.m. to 5 p.m.

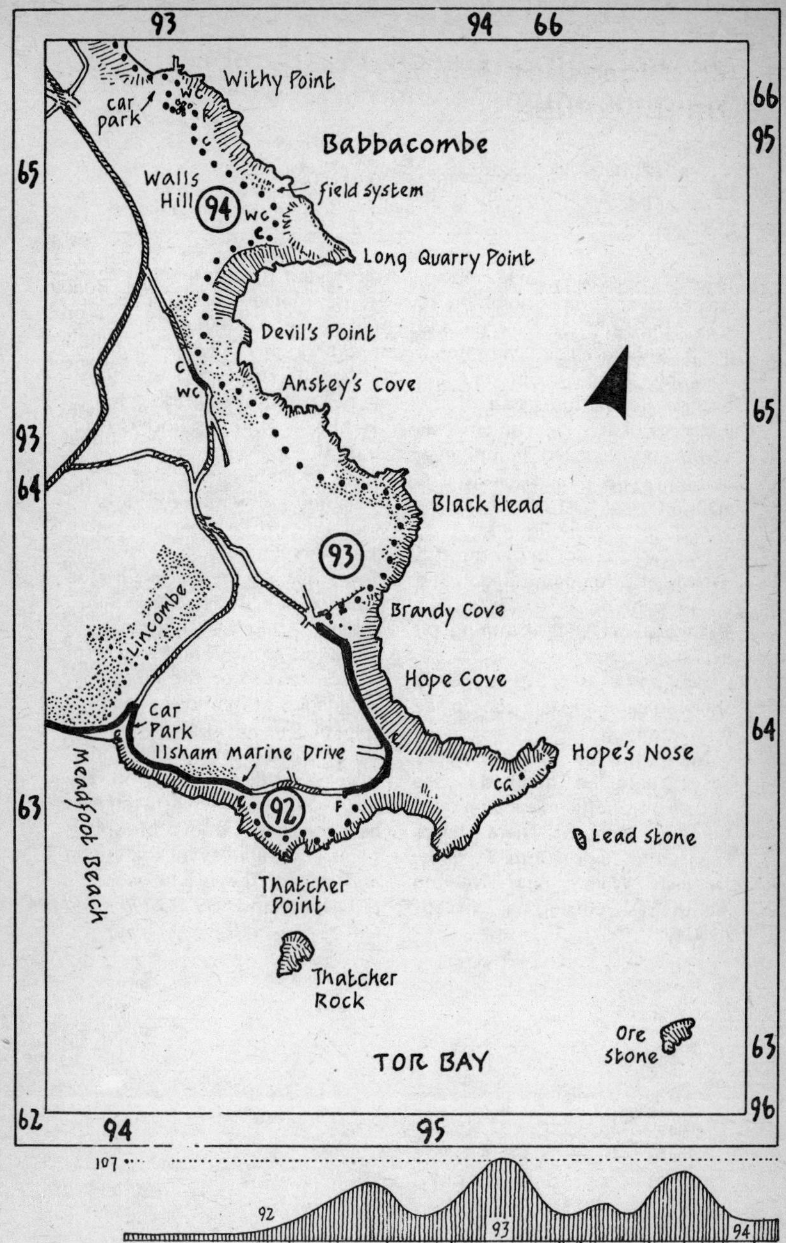

93
94 66
66
95
Withy Point
car park
wc
c
Babbacombe
Walls Hill
94
wc
field system
65
c
c
Long Quarry Point
Devil's Point
C
wc
Anstey's Cove
65
Black Head
93
93
93
64
Brandy Cove
Lincombe
Hope Cove
64
Car Park
Ilsham Marine Drive
Hope's Nose
Meadfoot Beach
C
Cg
92
F
63
Lead stone
Thatcher Point
Thatcher Rock
Ore stone
63
TOR BAY
62
94
95
96
107
Withy Point
92
93
94

26. Oddicombe Beach, Watcombe, Maidencombe, Mackerel Cove

3 miles
Maps: 1:25000 sheet SX86/96; 1:50000 sheet 202
Terrain: A gently undulating section through woods and along beaches.

St Marychurch, $\frac{1}{4}$ mile inland, was hit by a German bomb on 30 May 1943 and 21 children and teachers were killed. The church has now been rebuilt and the ancient Saxon font, one of the treasures of the old church, was saved and installed in the new building. This remarkable font is elaborately carved and depicts a number of strange figures.

The Path passes under the cliff railway at Oddicombe Beach and then climbs up alongside it for a short distance before turning off into the woods.

Watcombe Beach has gently shelving sand and is a good place for swimming.

Maidencombe has a grocer's shop, a café, the Thatched House pub, a post office, accommodation and campsites. There are bus services to Teignmouth, Torquay, Dawlish Warren and Newton Abbot. Early closing day is Wednesday.

Rudyard Kipling lived at Rock House, Maidencombe, in 1896–7 and wrote about his stay in his autobiography *Something of Myself*. He described the house as being '... almost too good to be true ... with big rooms each and all open to the sun, the grounds embellished with great trees and the warm land dipping southerly to the clear sea under the Marychurch cliffs'. But the house had a strange effect on the Kiplings and Rudyard was overcome with depression: 'a gathering blandness of mind and sorrow of heart – caused by the Feng-shui – the spirit of the house itself – a spirit of deep, deep despondency'. He wrote a Jamesian-like short story about the house called 'The House Surgeon'. While living here he conceived the idea of writing tracts and parables for the young and one of the results was the publication in 1899 of *Stalky and Co.*

92
93
94
69
STOKE-IN-TEIGN-HEAD 1
1¼ SHALDON
C
Mackerel Cove
Blackaller's Cove
97
K
C
WC
Maidencombe Beach
car park
Maidencombe
C
68
C
A 379
Shackley Bench
Bell Rock
BABBACOMBE
BAY
steps
S
96
car park
Valley of Rocks
Watcombe Head
WC
TORQUAY 1½
CS
Watcombe
Smuggler's Hole
67
Shag Cliff
Torquay
Golf Course
Roundhouse Point
95
St
Marychurch
WC
A
C
Petit Tor Point
steps
66
+
+
Oddicombe Beach
Cliff Railway
CC
Town
Hall
92
93
94
107
95
96
97

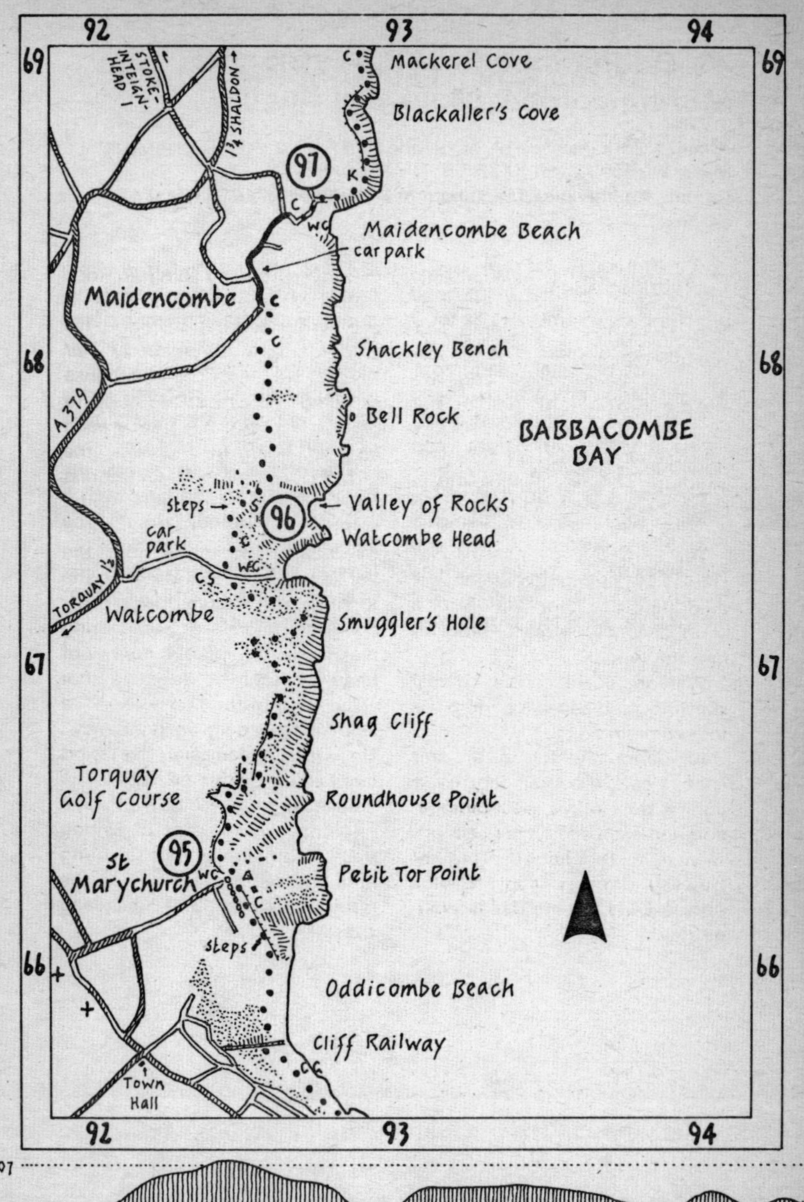

77

27. Herring Cove, Labrador Bay, Shaldon

3 miles
Maps: 1:25000 sheets SX86/96 and SX87/97; 1:50000 sheets 192 and 202
Terrain: An interesting and strenuous section with some fine views.

At Labrador Bay the Path meets the busy A379 on a sharp bend and follows the main road for $\frac{1}{4}$ mile. As there is no pavement, this is an extremely dangerous section and all walkers must exercise great caution. A stile and signpost leads off right and downhill to Shaldon.

Shaldon has a grocer's shop, cafés, restaurants, pubs, banks, a post office, accommodation and bus services to Torquay, Teignmouth, Dawlish Warren and Newton Abbot. Early closing day is Thursday. The modern-looking church of St Peter, near the bridge, was built at the turn of the century. The Homeyards Botanical Gardens contain many fine examples of sub-tropical plants which flourish in the mild climate of south Devon.

The official route across the River Teign is by the ferry, which operates frequently during the summer months until dusk. If the ferry is not operating, cross the river at Shaldon Bridge, which has a pavement.

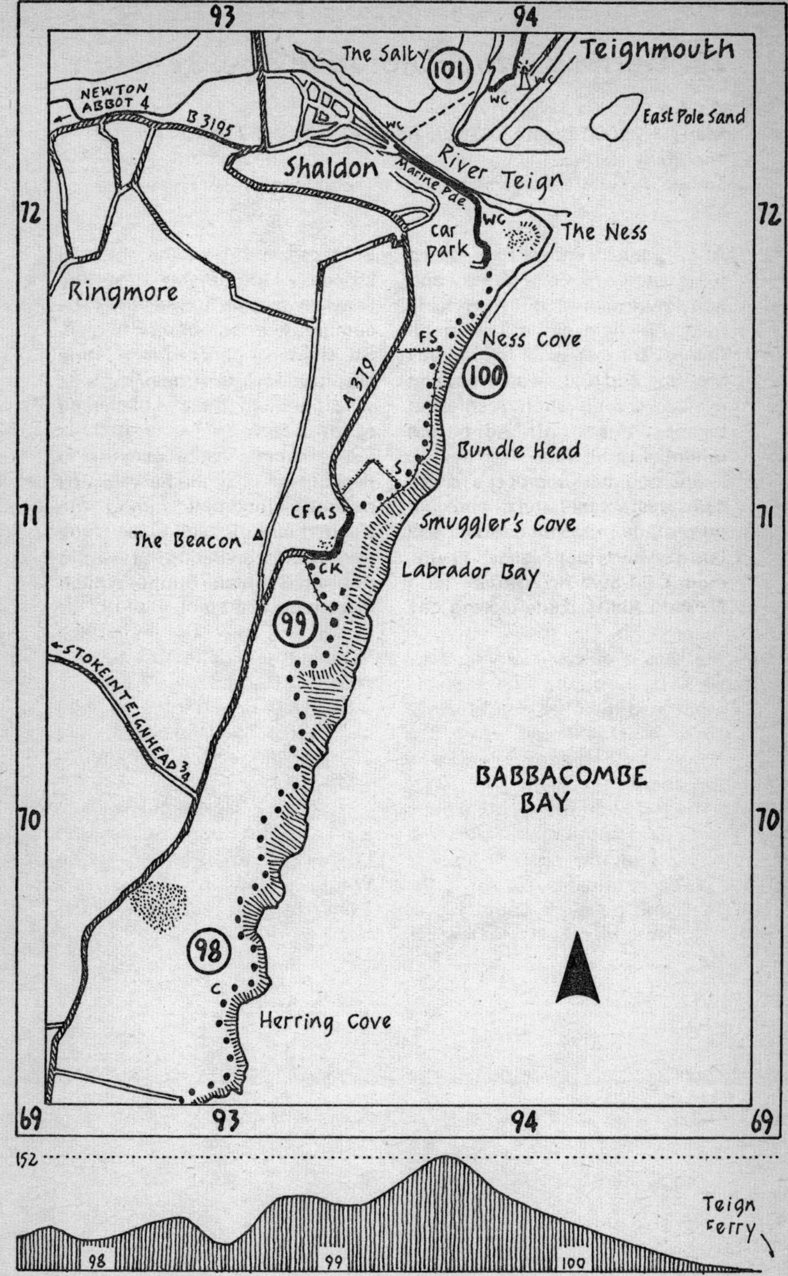

93
94
The Salty
101
Teignmouth
NEWTON ABBOT 4
B 3195
East Pole Sand
Shaldon
Marine Pde.
River Teign
72
72
WC
WC
WC
Car park
The Ness
Ringmore
FS
Ness Cove
100
A 379
Bundle Head
S
71
71
CFGS
Smuggler's Cove
The Beacon
CK
Labrador Bay
99
STOKEINTEIGNHEAD 3¾
BABBACOMBE BAY
70
70
98
C
Herring Cove
69
69
93
94
152
Teign Ferry
98
99
100

28. Teignmouth, Holcombe

2 miles
Maps: 1:25000 sheet SX87/97; 1:50000 sheets 192 and 202
Terrain: A low-level, uninspiring section alongside the railway.

During the high season, the 8 miles between Teignmouth and Starcross (mile 109) are probably not worth walking, as the route follows the sea wall, the railway and the road. Walkers arriving in Teignmouth should consider taking the bus or one of the infrequent trains to Starcross, or, at low tide, walk along the sands. Take Smugglers Lane inland, just before the Parson and Clerk Headland, which leads to the main road near Holcombe.

The official route across the River Teign is by the ferry, which operates a frequent service daily until dusk during the summer months. If the ferry is not operating, walkers should cross the bridge to Shaldon. There is a pavement.

Teignmouth has a population of 12,000 and all the facilities of a town of this size. There is a Tourist Information Office at the Den, and there are train services to Plymouth, Exeter, Dawlish, Starcross and Torquay, and bus services to Bishopsteignton, Dawlish Warren, Exeter, Maidencombe, Newton Abbot, Shaldon, Starcross and Torquay. Early closing day is Thursday.

Teignmouth has a splendid sandy beach and is a popular family resort. Den Crescent was laid out in 1826 and is still the most attractive part of the town. John Keats finished his long poem *Endymion* and sent it to his publishers while living for a short time at 20 Northumberland Place in 1818. Fanny Burney visited frequently and Jane Austen came here in 1802. The town is ancient: it has a seal dating from the reign of Ethelred the Unready (1002) and is mentioned in a charter of 1044.

Holcombe has a grocer's shop, a post office, public houses and bus services to Torquay, Dawlish Warren, Newton Abbot and Exeter. Early closing day is Thursday.

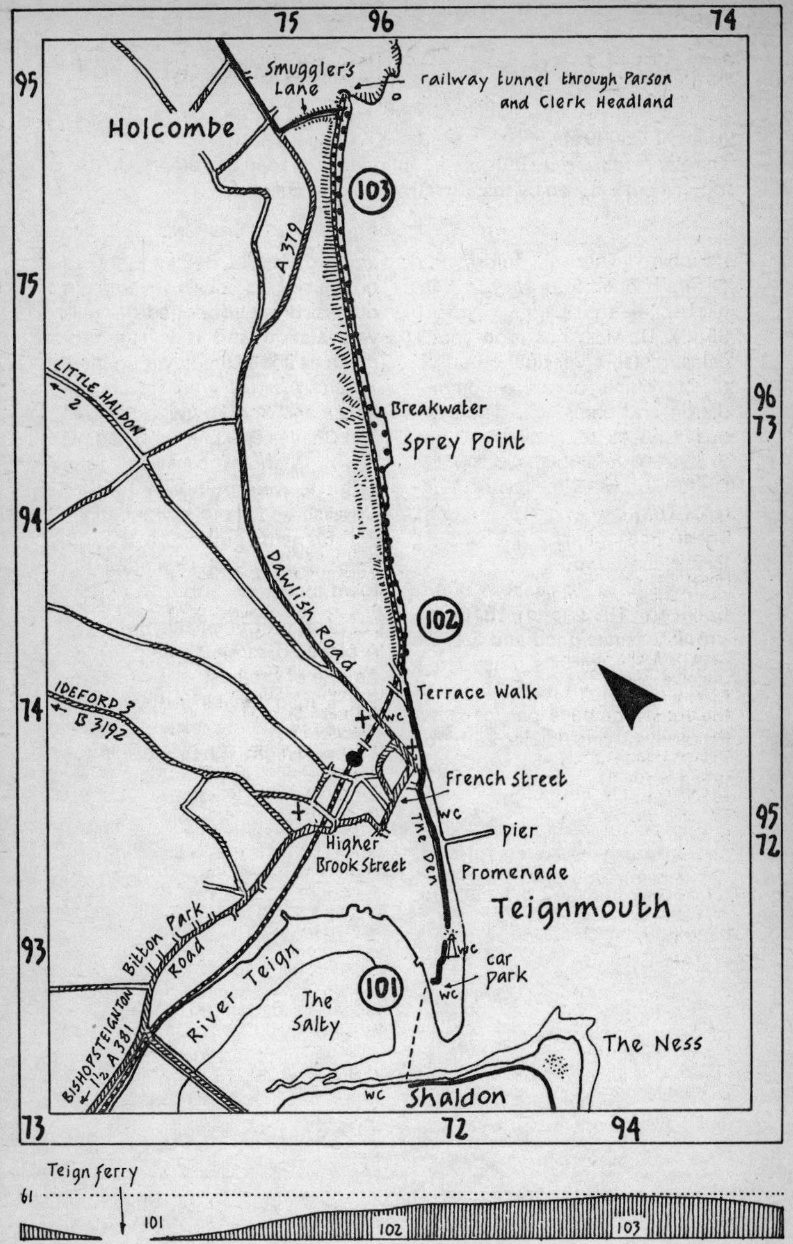

75
96
74
95
Smuggler's Lane
railway tunnel through Parson and Clerk Headland
Holcombe
103
A 379
75
LITTLE HALDON
2
Breakwater
Sprey Point
96
73
Dawlish Road
94
IDEFORD 3
B 3192
74
102
Terrace Walk
wc
French Street
wc
95
72
pier
Higher Brook Street
The Den
Promenade
Teignmouth
Bilton Park Road
93
River Teign
The Salty
101
wc
car park
wc
BISHOPSTEIGNTON
1½ A 381
The Ness
73
wc
Shaldon
72
94
Teign ferry
61
101
102
103

29. East Down, Dawlish, Langstone Rock

3 miles
Maps: 1:25000 sheet SX87/97; 1:50000 sheet 192
Terrain: Another very dull stretch following the road and alongside the railway but relieved by the attractive resort of Dawlish.

Dawlish Tourist Information Centre is open from May to September at the Lawn (Dawlish 3589). Dawlish has food shops, cafés, restaurants, public houses, a post office, banks, accommodation and campsites. There are bus services to Newton Abbot, Exeter, Ashcombe, Cockwood, Doddiscombsleigh, Dawlish Warren, Torquay and Teignmouth. There are trains to Torquay, Exeter and London.

Dawlish is of Saxon origin. Between 1803 and 1810 the Brook was realigned and a series of artificial waterfalls constructed. This area, known as the Lawn, is the most attractive part of Dawlish and still has houses with iron balconies and bow windows. Brook House and Manor House are two elegant Regency houses now used as local government offices. Brunel designed the railway station and it is still very much as it was the day it opened.

Jane Austen, who set part of *Sense and Sensibility*, in the area and Charles Dickens, who had his young Nicholas Nickleby grow up here, were both very fond of Dawlish, and another writer, Richard Barham, author of the *Ingoldsby Legends*, described the town thus:

. . . pleasant but smallish,
A place I'd suggest
As one of the best
For a man breaking down who needs absolute rest,
Especially, too, if he's weak in the chest.

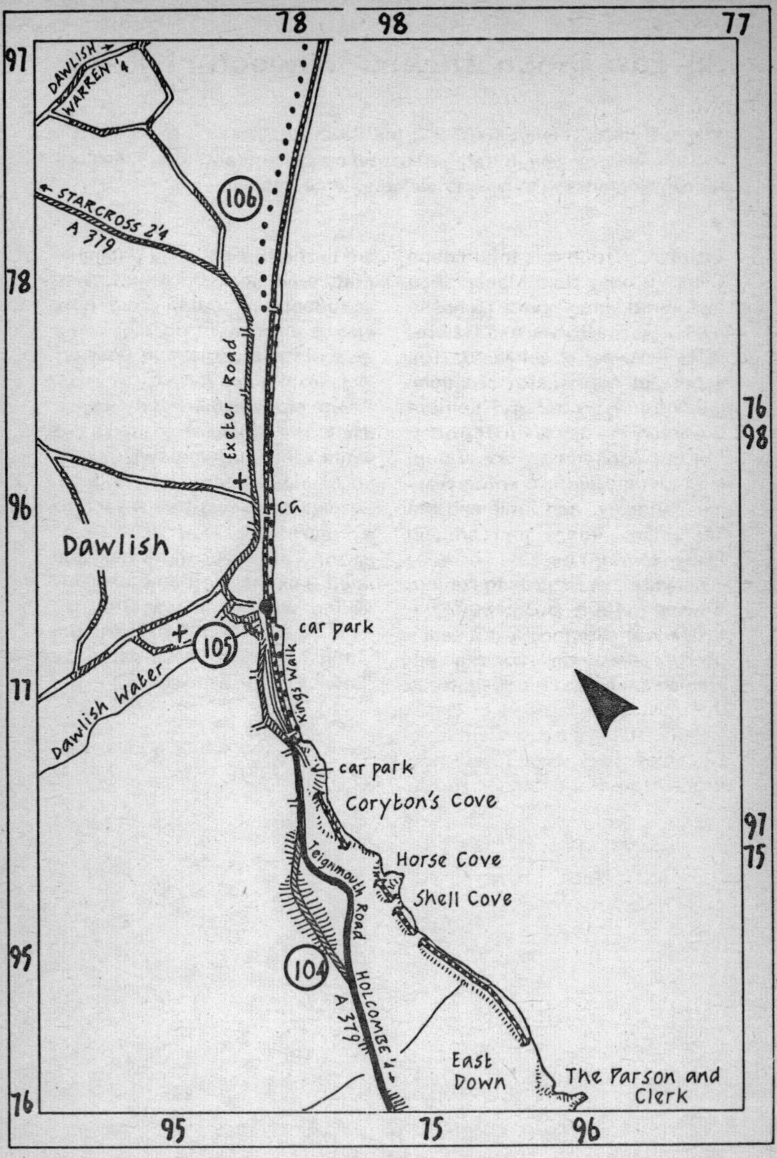

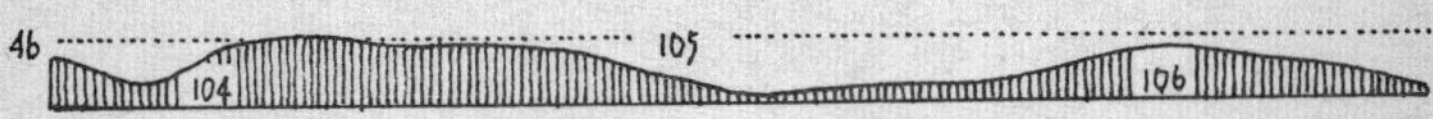

97
78
98
77
DAWLISH WARREN ¼
← STARCROSS 2¼ A 379
106
Exeter Road
78
76
98
Dawlish
ca
96
car park
105
Dawlish Water
77
car park
Kings Walk
Coryton's Cove
97
75
Horse Cove
Teignmouth Road
Shell Cove
104
HOLCOMBE ¼
A 379
95
East Down
The Parson and Clerk
76
95
75
96
46
104
105
106

30. Langstone Rock, Cockwood

3 miles
Maps: 1:25000 sheets SX87/97 and SX88/98; 1:50000 sheet 192
Terrain: Another very miserable section almost entirely along roads but adjacent to a fascinating and varied wildlife habitat.

Dawlish Warren has food shops, cafés, public house, a post office, accommodation and a campsite. There are bus services to Newton Abbot, Exeter, Cockwood, Torquay and Teignmouth, and trains to Torquay, Exeter and London. Early closing day is on Thursday.

Cockwood has a grocer's shop, a pub (the Ship Inn at Starcross, recommended for food and real ale by Egon Ronay) and camping. Early closing day is Thursday. There are bus services to Newton Abbot, Exeter and Dawlish.

Dawlish Warren is not just a golf course, caravan site and shanty town; the mudflats to the north form part of a National Nature Reserve. Cord grass was introduced in 1935 and now grows extensively on the inland side of the mud flats, as does eel grass and glasswort.

The Exe estuary is now a National Wildfowl Reserve. A wide variety of wildfowl, including large flocks of wigeon, waders, terns and swans such as Bewicks and Whoopers, can be seen. The brackish water and mud flats are the home of interesting water plant varieties, including the sea club rush and the attractive michaelmas-daisy-like flowers of the sea aster.

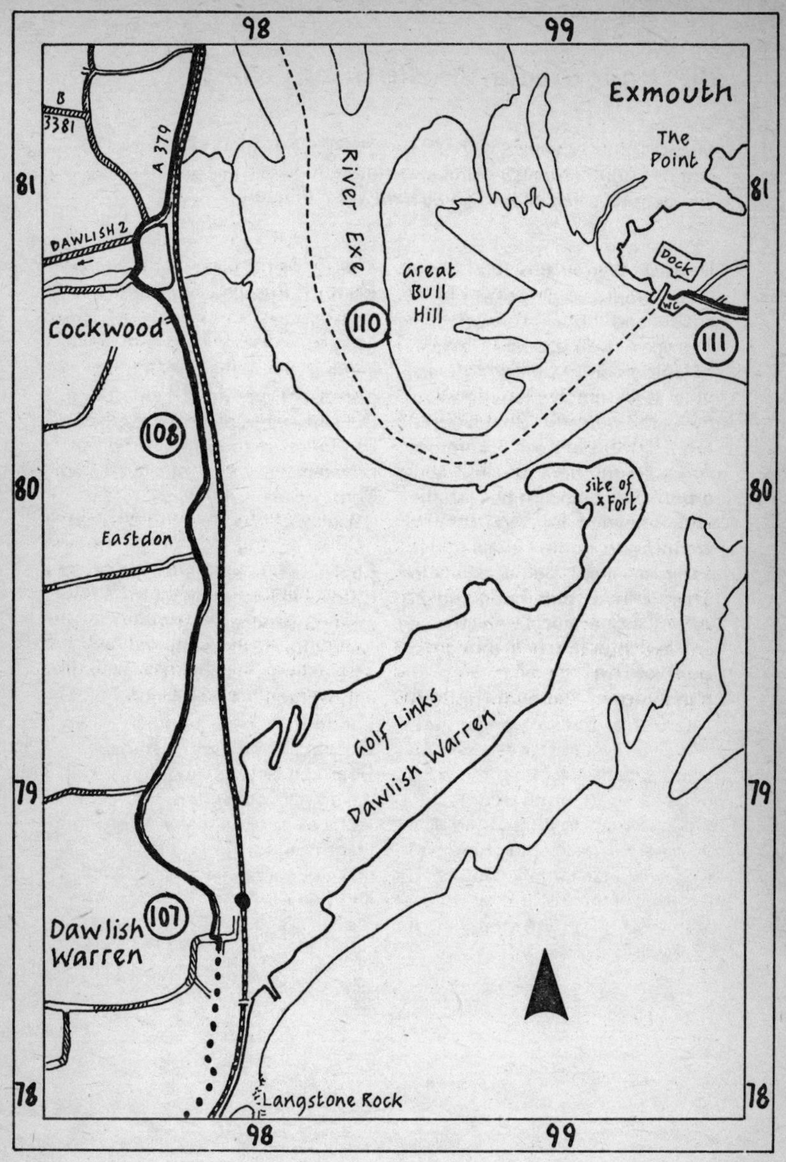
98
99
Exmouth
The Point
B 3381
A 379
81
81
River Exe
Dock
DAWLISH 2
Great Bull Hill
110
WC
111
Cockwood
108
site of x Fort
80
80
Eastdon
Golf Links
Dawlish Warren
79
79
Dawlish Warren
107
78
78
Langstone Rock
98
99
15
107
108

31. Starcross, Exmouth

3 miles
Maps: 1:25000 sheets SX87/97 and SY08/18; 1:50000 sheet 192
Terrain: Another urban section with much road walking but including a pleasant crossing of the Exe by ferry.

Starcross has a grocer's shop, public houses, a post office, banks and bus services to Newton Abbot, Exeter, Dawlish and Teignmouth. Its sailing club, founded in the eighteenth century, is the oldest in Britain.

The ferry between Starcross and Exmouth operates seasonally from May to September. If the ferry is not operating (phone Exmouth 72009 for exact dates and times) it will be necessary to go by train or bus, changing at Exeter. Only a few trains stop at Torcross, but the bus service is fairly frequent.

On reaching Exmouth (or Starcross if the ferry is operating), walkers travelling west should decide whether to take the train or bus to Teignmouth or Brixham, or even as far as Kingswear. The 40 miles between Starcross and Kingswear is largely dull and urbanized, much of it over roads, with only one or two stretches of good walking. See p. 9.

A good case can be made for taking the bus or train as far as Torquay or Paignton. From Torquay there is a ferry service in summer to Brixham which makes a pleasant trip. From Paignton, in the summer, a pleasant excursion can be made to Kingswear on the privately owned steam-hauled Torbay Steam Railway.

Exmouth (population 26,000) has shops, cafés, restaurants, public houses, banks, a post office and accommodation. There are bus services to Withycombe, Sandy Bay, Sidmouth and Exeter, and train services to Exeter with connections to Torquay and London. It is a popular family seaside resort with some fine Georgian houses, some of which have been converted into hotels, and has a particularly fine nineteenth-century church. Nearby, on the Beacon, lived Lady Nelson and Lady Byron.

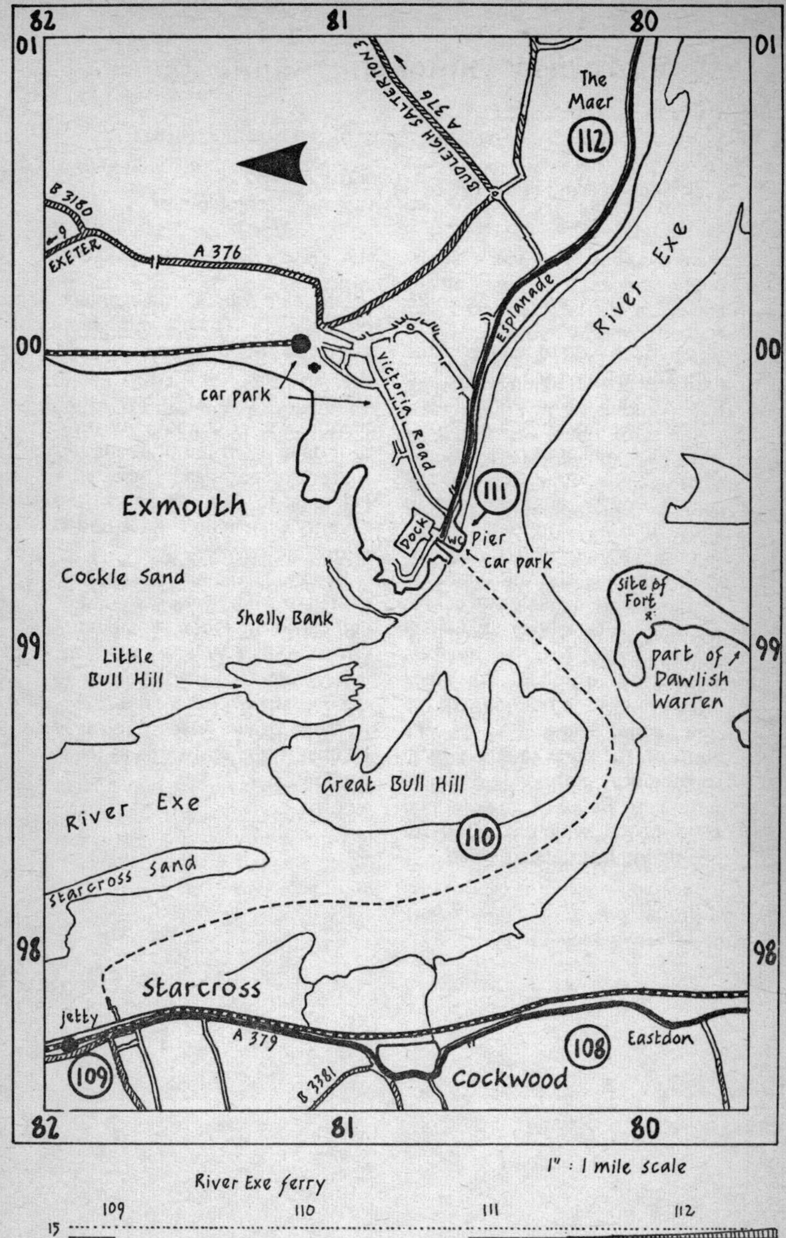

82
81
80
01
01
The Maer
112
BUDLEIGH SALTERTON 3
A 376
B 3180
9
EXETER
A 376
River Exe
00
00
car park
Victoria Road
Esplanade
Exmouth
111
Pier
car park
Dock
wc
Cockle Sand
Site of Fort
x
Shelly Bank
99
99
Little Bull Hill
part of Dawlish Warren
Great Bull Hill
River Exe
110
Starcross Sand
98
98
Starcross
jetty
A 379
Eastdon
109
108
B 3381
Cockwood
82
81
80
1" : 1 mile scale
River Exe ferry
109
110
111
112
15

32. Exmouth Promenade, Sandy Bay, West Down Beacon

3 miles
Maps: 1:25000 sheet SY08/18; 1:50000 sheet 192
Terrain: Good cliff-top walking with a strenuous climb out of Littleham Cove.

At the eastern end of Exmouth promenade there are two sets of steps which lead to the top of the cliff. Those from the beach will be covered by the sea at high tide.

The rifle range at Straight Point forces the walker to pass through the unsightly litter of caravans at Sandy Bay. It is impossible to show the route in detail. East-bound walkers should walk towards the sea and the boundary hedge, where a stile gives access to the cliffs above Littleham Cove. West-bound walkers should try to follow the fence which marks the boundary of the rifle range. There is a grocer's shop on the caravan site as well as a café. A path leads down to Littleham Cove, a shingle and sand beach which is good for swimming but gets crowded.

Littleham lies $\frac{1}{2}$ mile inland off the Path. The church, dedicated to St Margaret and St Andrew, was the ancient parish church of Exmouth. It has a thirteenth-century chancel but most of it dates from the fifteenth and sixteenth centuries. There is a memorial to Lady Nelson in the Chantry Chapel and she is buried in the churchyard.

Beyond Littleham Cove is a stretch of wild, overgrown under-cliff called the Floors, a habitat of whitethroats. Willow warblers, yellowhammers, goldfinches and the occasional buzzard nest there. At West Down Beacon you may be able to see eastwards as far as Portland Bill.

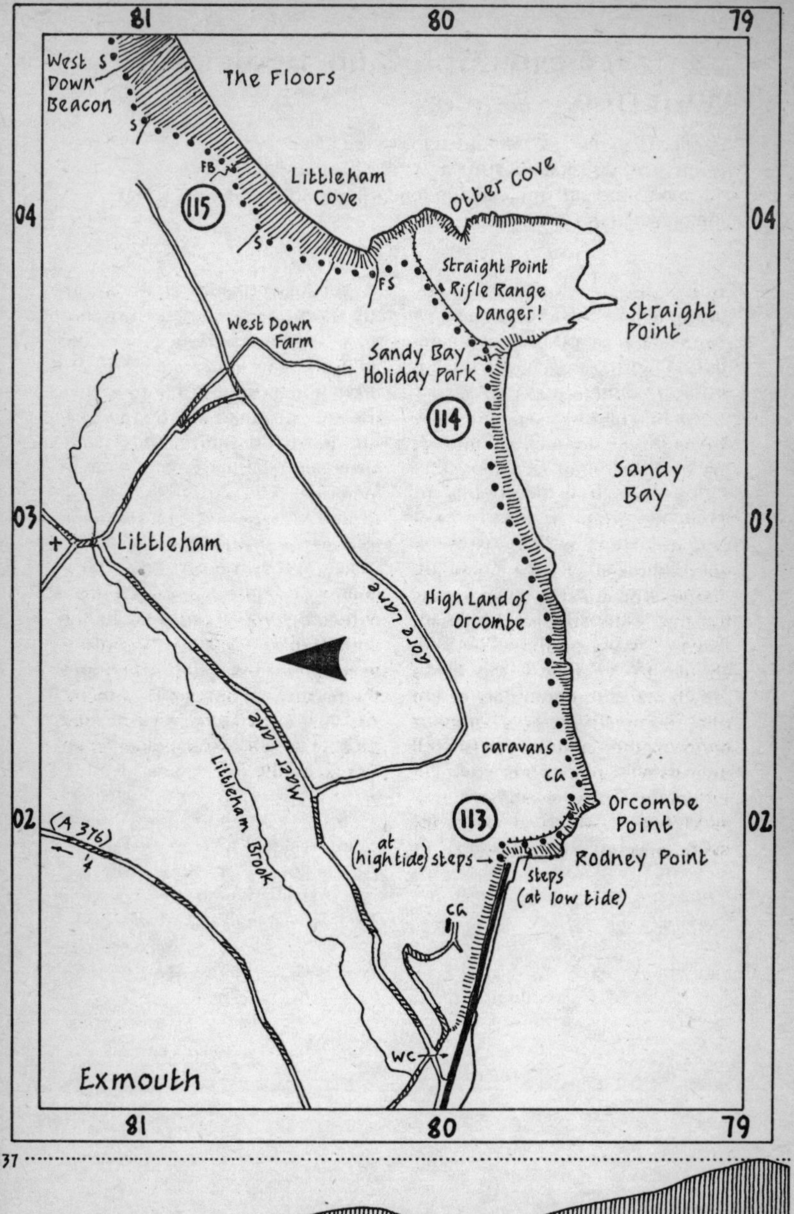

81
80
79
West Down Beacon
S
S
The Floors
FB
115
Littleham Cove
S
S
FS
Otter Cove
Straight Point Rifle Range Danger!
Straight Point
04
04
West Down Farm
Sandy Bay Holiday Park
114
Sandy Bay
03
Littleham
High Land of Orcombe
Gore Lane
03
+
Meer Lane
caravans
CG
Orcombe Point
02
(A 376)
Littleham Brook
113
at (high tide) steps →
Rodney Point
steps (at low tide)
02
CG
WC →
Exmouth
81
80
79
137
30
113
114
115

33. East Devon Golf Club, Budleigh Salterton

3 miles (2½ miles via the ford at the river Otter)
Maps: 1:25000 sheet SY08/18; 1:50000 sheet 192
Terrain: Good cliff-top walking followed by an inland walk along the banks of the River Otter.

Budleigh Salterton has shops, cafés, restaurants, public houses, banks, a post office, accommodation and bus services to Exmouth, Sidmouth, Exeter and Knowle. The town has a delightful air of faded gentility. Sensitive walkers will feel gross as they stride through in their boots and breeches.

Brave souls wishing to avoid the detour inland to cross the River Otter may be able to ford the river at low tide. Cross at the narrowest point where the cliffs come down to the river and hug them on the inland side. The water is waist-deep at this point, but in normal conditions there is no current and it shoals rapidly. East-bound walkers should not attempt to cross on the seaward side of the cliffs as there is no way up them to reach the Path. Fording the river is *not* recommended.

East Budleigh, 1 mile inland, has many associations with Sir Walter Raleigh. The church of All Saints, in which he worshipped, is mostly fifteenth-century, but the north aisle is thirteenth-century. The doors are 500 years old and the finely carved pews are from the sixteenth century. The Raleigh pews are the first two on the left-hand side of the middle aisle and bear the Raleigh coat of arms.

One mile west of East Budleigh is Hayes Barton, the birthplace of Raleigh. The house remains remarkably little changed from when Sir Walter knew it in the middle of the sixteenth century. It is open on weekday afternoons from June to mid-September.

The Italian Gardens at Bicton (2¼ miles north of Budleigh Salterton on the A376; open daily 10 a.m. to 6 p.m. from Easter to October) include the James Countryside Museum, a narrow-gauge railway and a pinetum laid out in 1840 which now contains excellent specimens of rare conifers. There are five glasshouses, an American garden and temples and conservatories.

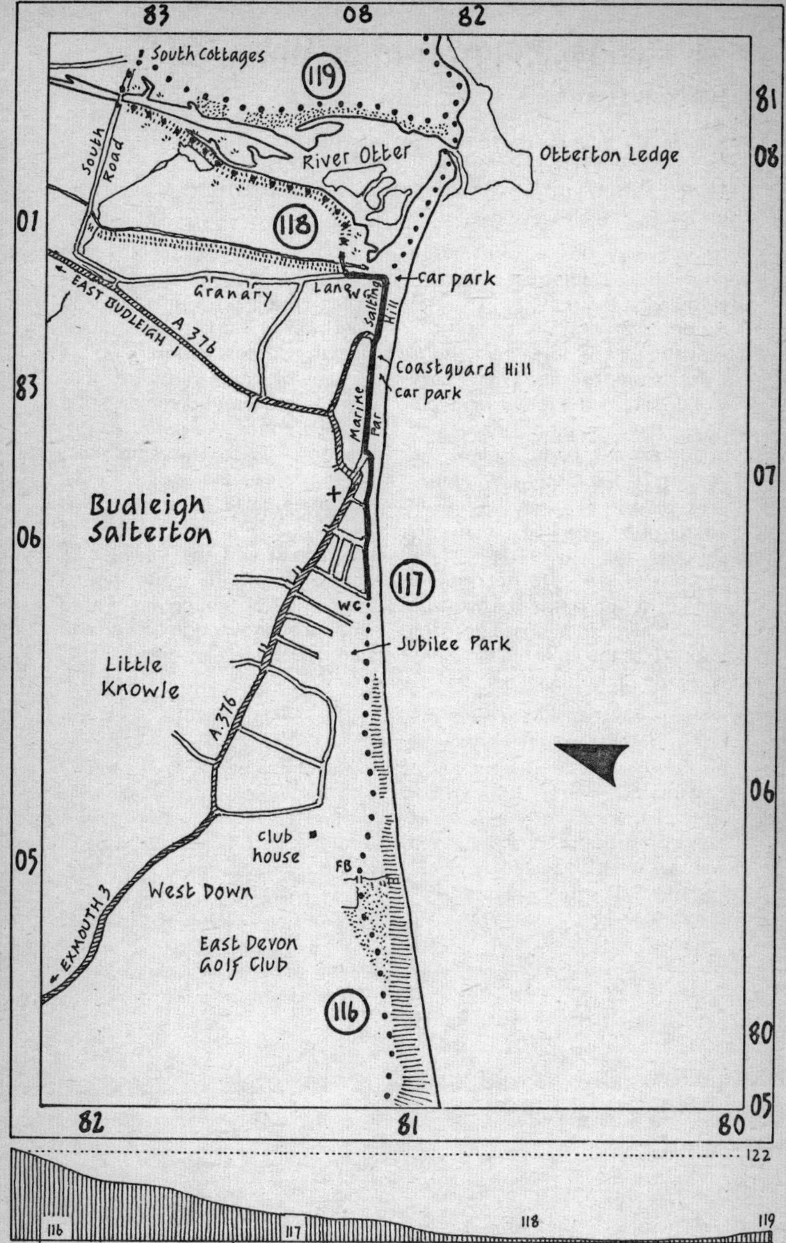

83
08
82
South Cottages
119
River Otter
Otterton Ledge
81
08
South Road
01
118
car park
Granary
Lane
WC
Salting Hill
83
A 376
EAST BUDLEIGH 1
Coastguard Hill
car park
Marine Par
07
Budleigh
Salterton
06
117
WC
Jubilee Park
Little
Knowle
A 376
EXMOUTH 3
05
club
house
West Down
FB
East Devon
Golf Club
116
80
05
82
81
80
116
117
118
119
122

34. Danger Point, Brandy Head, Ladram Bay

$2\frac{1}{2}$ miles
Maps: 1:25000 sheet SY08/18; 1:50000 sheet 192
Terrain: Splendid cliff-top walking with one steep descent.

Ladram Bay has a café and a public house. Its great attraction is the splendid rock scenery. The action of the sea on the soft red sandstone has detached huge blocks from the cliffs which have weathered and eroded and are now the roosting places of countless sea birds. Before the coming of the motor car, gentlemen used to bathe in the buff at Ladram Bay. The beach is mainly shingle, but there are some patches of sand. Do not venture too far to the east or the west on a flood tide. It is possible to be trapped, as the cliffs are too steep and crumbling to climb.

During the eighteenth and nineteenth centuries the area between Budleigh Salterton and Beer was a nest of smugglers. Captain Marryat, author of a number of naval yarns for children, was once in command of a revenue cutter and patrolled this section of coast. The remoteness of the area, the existence of numerous small bays and caves for the landing and hiding of contraband and the treacherous tides and currents made this an ideal area for smuggling. Those with local knowledge had a head start over the excise men.

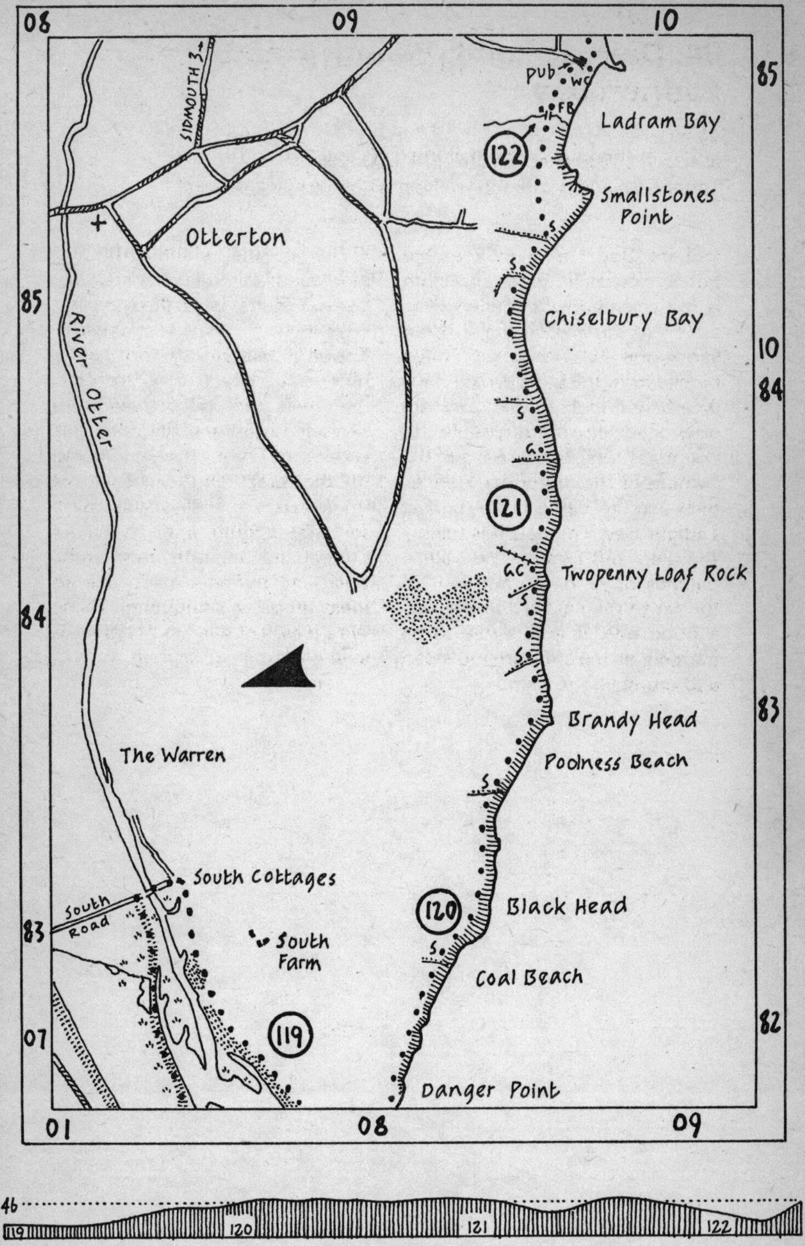

08
09
10
85
SIDMOUTH 3
pub
wc
FB
Ladram Bay
122
Smallstones Point
Chiselbury Bay
85
Otterton
River Otter
10
84
S
G
121
GC
S
Twopenny Loaf Rock
S
84
S
Brandy Head
83
Poolness Beach
S
The Warren
South Cottages
South Road
83
South Farm
120
Black Head
S
Coal Beach
119
07
82
Danger Point
01
08
09

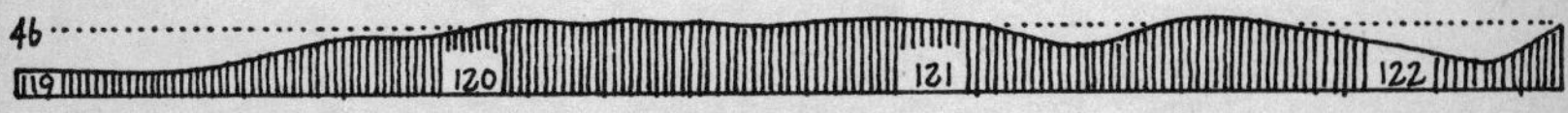

46
119
120
121
122

35. Sandy Cove, Sidmouth

3 miles
Maps: 1:25000 sheets SY08/18 and SY29/39; 1:50000 sheet 192
Terrain: A strenuous section along cliffs and through woods.

West-bound walkers must be careful not to miss the kissing gate which leads into the wood on the left-hand side of the lane at mile 123.

Sidmouth has shops, cafés, restaurants, public houses, banks, a post office, accommodation and bus services to Seaton, Lyme Regis, Exmouth, Sidbury, Ottery St Mary and Honiton.

Once a flourishing port, rivalling in importance both Plymouth and Dartmouth, the town reverted to a small fishing village when the River Sid silted up. Sidmouth's fortunes revived during the Georgian period, when it became a fashionable watering place. It still retains a Regency atmosphere and the elegant terraces are well worth looking at. The infant Victoria and her impoverished parents the Duke and Duchess of Kent came here to escape creditors in 1819 and resided at Woolbrook Cottage, now the Royal Glen Hotel. The Duke died within a few months of his arrival and the Duchess used to take Victoria on to the front and tell people that they were looking at a future Queen of England.

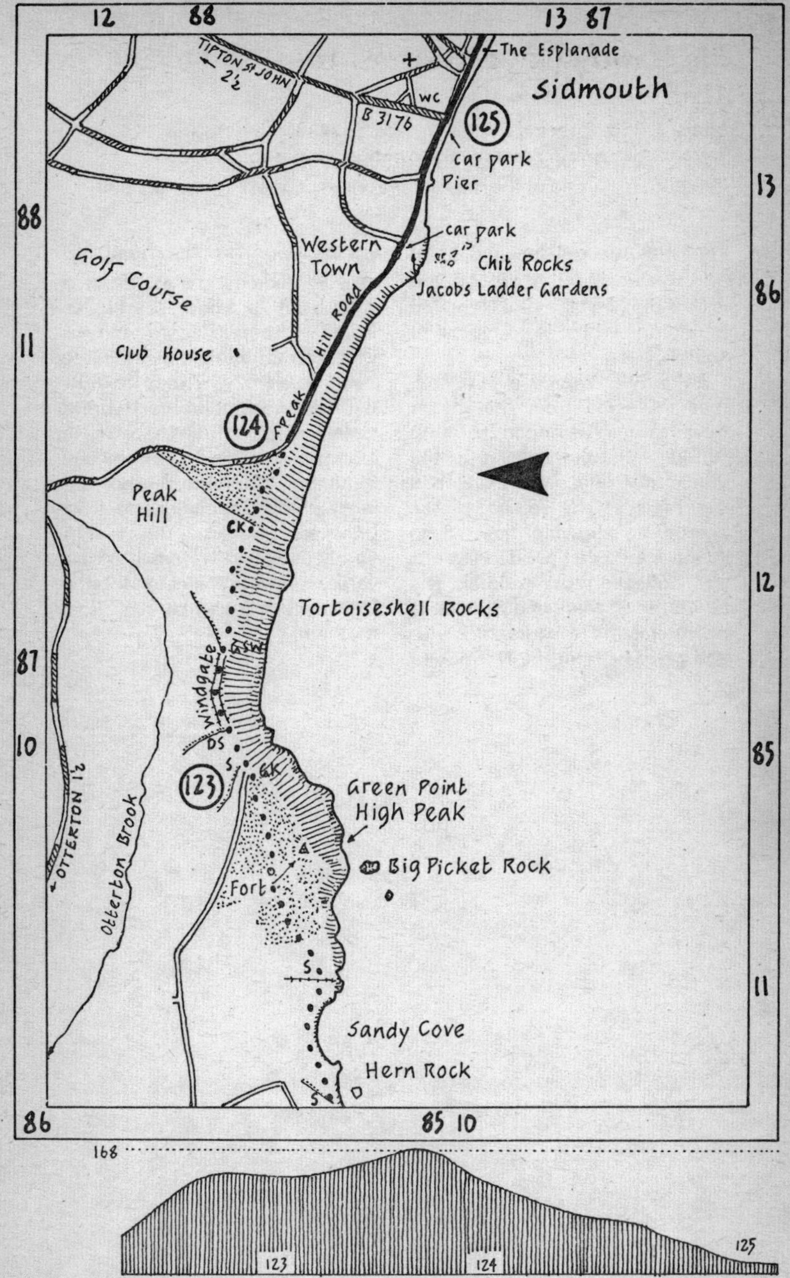

12
88
13 87
TIPTON St JOHN 2½
The Esplanade
Sidmouth
WC
B 3176
125
car park
Pier
13
88
Golf Course
Western Town
car park
Chit Rocks
Jacobs Ladder Gardens
86
11
Club House
124
Freak Hill Road
Peak Hill
CK
12
Tortoiseshell Rocks
87
GSW
Windgate
DS
10
S
123
CK
85
Green Point
High Peak
Fort
Big Picket Rock
OTTERTON 1½
Otterton Brook
11
S
Sandy Cove
Hern Rock
S
86
85 10
168
123
124
125

36. River Sid, Salcombe Mouth, Lower Dunscombe Cliff

$3\frac{1}{2}$ miles
Maps: 1:25000 sheet SY29/39; 1:50000 sheet 192
Terrain: This is one of the most strenuous sections of the whole path.

The cliffs rise to over five hundred feet on this stretch of coast and it is here that we leave the New Red Sandstone which is so typical of south Devon.

Salcombe Regis, a mile inland, gets its name from the manor which once belonged to King Alfred. Athelstan gave it to the monks of Exeter, who developed salt pans at the mouth of the combe by allowing the sea to evaporate in shallow depressions and collecting the residue. The church of St Mary and St Peter is an interesting mixture of styles and periods, from the Norman to the Perpendicular. The fifteenth-century lectern, carved from a solid block of wood, was hidden from the Roundheads during the Civil War. There is a memorial to Joanna Avant, who died in 1695, with an inscription in Hebrew, Greek, Latin and English. Sir Norman Lockyer, the eminent Victorian astronomer who developed many theories about the universe, is buried in the churchyard. His attractive, small observatory is now in the care of Exeter University and can be seen from the Path.

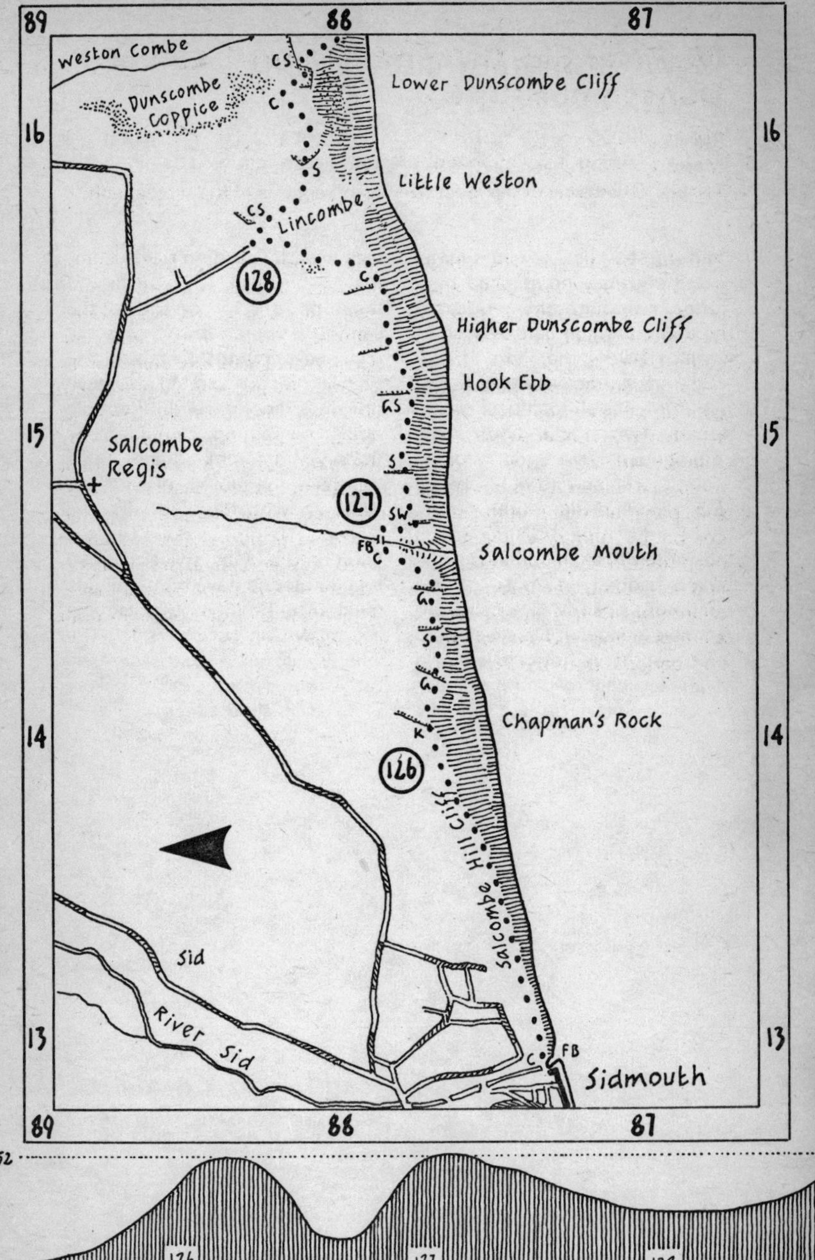

89
88
87
16
16
Weston Combe
CS
Dunscombe
Coppice
C
Lower Dunscombe Cliff
S
Little Weston
CS
Lincombe
128
C
Higher Dunscombe Cliff
Hook Ebb
GS
15
15
Salcombe
Regis
S
127
SW
FB
C
Salcombe Mouth
G
S
G
14
14
K
Chapman's Rock
126
Salcombe Hill Cliff
Sid
13
13
River Sid
C
FB
Sidmouth
89
88
87
152
126
127
128

37. Weston Mouth, Berry Cliff

2½ miles
Maps: 1:25000 sheet SY29/39; 1:50000 sheet 192
Terrain: A strenuous climb out of Weston Mouth followed by high cliff-top walking.

Branscombe lies a little way inland and may be reached by a footpath through the woods to the church which can be seen in a valley below the Path. It is a scattered, attractive village and has a grocer's shop, a post office, a café, two public houses recommended by Egon Ronay, accommodation and bus services to Seaton and Sidmouth.

The church of St Winefreda is most interesting. It contains some Saxon work, but most of the building is Early English and Norman in style. It has a splendid Jacobean carved oak gallery and a rare eighteenth-century three-decker pulpit. The lower deck was used for reading the lessons, the middle deck for prayers and the top deck for preaching the sermon. There are traces of medieval paintings, including one with a scene depicting the devil driving a lance through a couple doing something forbidden by the seventh commandment. Joan Wadham, the mother of Nicholas Wadham who founded Wadham College, Oxford, is buried in the church. She was twice married and reputed to have borne twenty children, although only seventeen are shown on her memorial. The village still has an old-fashioned blacksmith's forge and a bakery with wood-fired ovens.

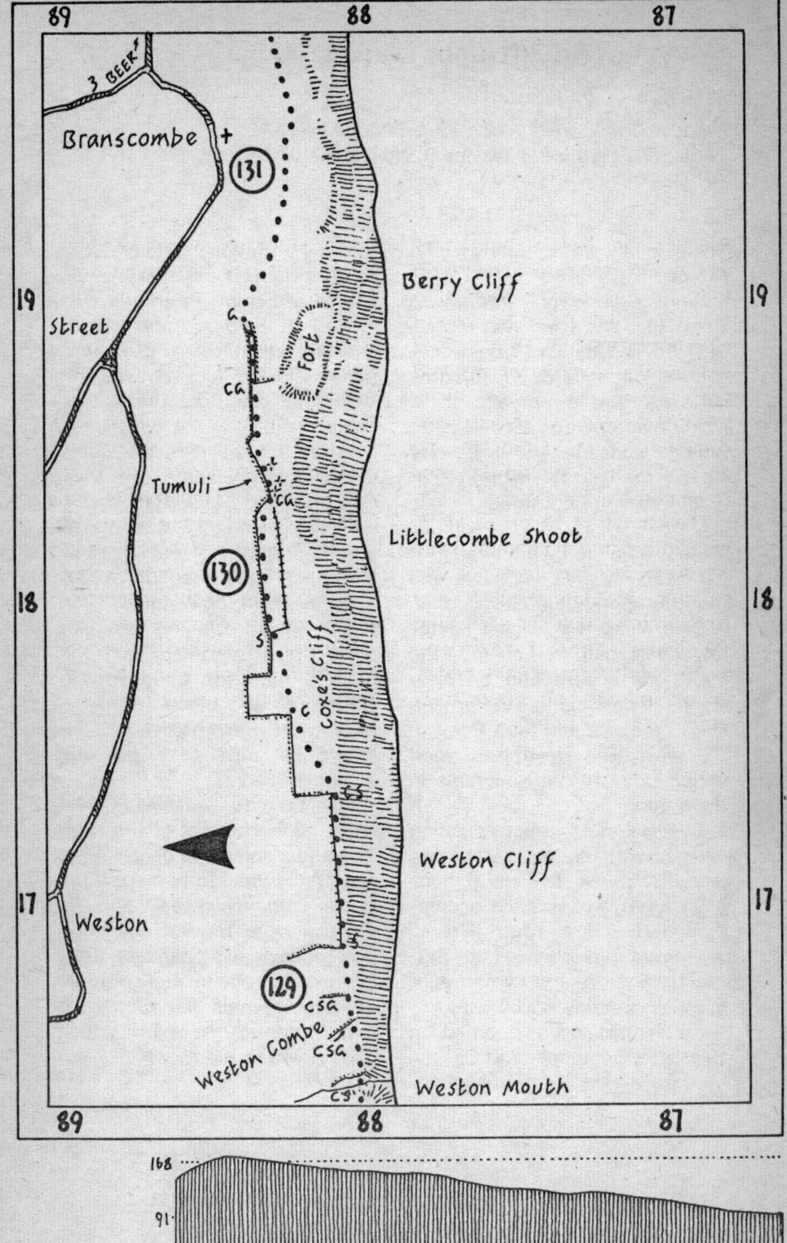

89
88
87
3 BEER
Branscombe
131
Berry Cliff
19
Street
Fort
Tumuli
Littlecombe Shoot
130
18
Coxe's Cliff
Weston Cliff
17
Weston
129
Weston Combe
Weston Mouth
89
88
87
168
91
129
130
131

38. Branscombe Mouth, Beer Head, Beer

$3\frac{1}{2}$ miles
Maps: 1:25000 sheet SY29/39; 1:50000 sheet 192
Terrain: This is another exceptionally strenuous section.

There is a café at Branscombe Mouth.

From Branscombe Mouth to Beer Head there are two routes. Just beyond mile 132 there is a stile which leads down to some caravans and eventually to a rather overgrown undercliff path, which suddenly climbs very steeply to rejoin the main Path at a stile near the coastguard look-out on Beer Head. The official route is much to be preferred as it has such magnificent views and glorious springy turf.

Beer Head is the most southerly chalk cliff in England, the views are superb and on clear days it is possible to see Portland Bill to the east and Start Point to the west. The Head is a good watch point for bird migrants in the autumn.

Beer is a most attractive fishing village, with shops, cafés, restaurants, public houses, a bank (part-time), a post office, accommodation and a Youth Hostel. There are bus services to Sidmouth, Seaton, and Lyme Regis. Early closing day is Thursday.

Stone has been quarried at Beer for centuries and is the material from which Exeter Cathedral is built. It has the unusual quality of being soft and easy to cut — it hardens only when exposed to the air. Beer was famous for its lace and Queen Victoria's wedding dress was made from it. The village was the haunt of smugglers in the eighteenth and nineteenth centuries. One of them, Jack Rattenbury, who was born in 1778, wrote an autobiography, *Memoirs of a Smuggler*, published in 1837. After a most adventurous life, which included being captured by Spanish privateers and the French, tried for smuggling in Dartmouth and pressed into the navy, from which he deserted, he ended his days as a peaceful fisherman.

East-bound wayfarers will arrive at the bottom of the High Street just above the beach. They should continue forward past the public conveniences and a German mine (now a collecting box for seamen's charities). Turn left, pass the shelter and continue forward towards the big white cliff, ignoring the path which goes down to the beach.

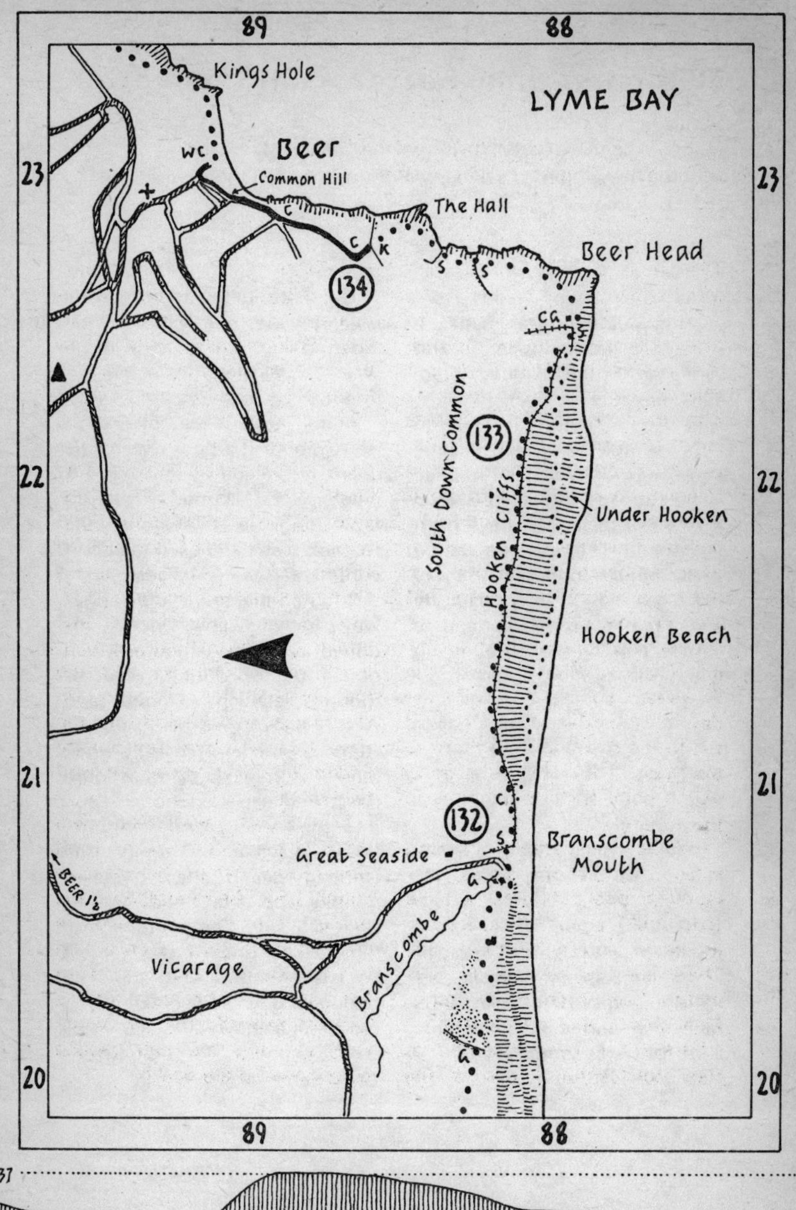

89
88
Kings Hole
LYME BAY
23
23
wc
Beer
Common Hill
The Hall
Beer Head
c
c
k
s
s
134
CG
South Down Common
133
Hooken cliffs
Under Hooken
22
22
Hooken Beach
21
21
c
132
s
Great Seaside
Branscombe
Mouth
BEER 1½
G
Vicarage
Branscombe
G
20
20
89
88
137
132
133
134

39. Seaton Hole, Seaton, Golf Course

3 miles
Maps: 1:25000 sheet SY29/39; 1:50000 sheet 192.
Terrain: This section is rather urban in character but there are some pleasant views.

Seaton has shops, cafés, restaurants, public houses, banks, a post office, accommodation and campsites on the Axmouth road. There are bus services to Beer, Lyme Regis, Sidmouth, Honiton and Taunton, and an electric tramway to Colyford.

The Romans settled in Seaton and two of their villas have been unearthed. The parish church dates from the fourteenth century and has a fifteenth-century tower. It contains an epitaph to John Starre with the following punning inscription:

> Starr on Hie!
> Where should a starr be
> But on Hie?
> Tho underneath
> He now doth lie,
> Sleeping in dust,
> Yet shall he rise
> More glorious than
> Starres in the skies.

Semi-precious stones such as beryls, garnets, agates and jaspers may sometimes be picked up on the beach and it is a favourite place for beachcombers.

The Path follows the private road to the golf club. When crossing the links, considerate walkers will take care not to interrupt any games in progress.

At the eastern end of Seaton is Axmouth harbour, with the charming village of that name $\frac{1}{4}$ mile inland. Axmouth was a flourishing port before the Romans came and used to import continental wares. These were distributed inland via the Ridgeway Path, which once continued as far as Axmouth. Much of its route can still be traced, although between Axmouth and Avebury it is largely metalled. The Romans made Axmouth their most important port on the south coast and exported from it iron from the Mendips and wool from the Cotswolds. During the Norman period there were a number of cliff falls and the harbour silted up. The bridge across the Axe is one of the earliest known examples of a concrete bridge and is a piece of living industrial archaeology.

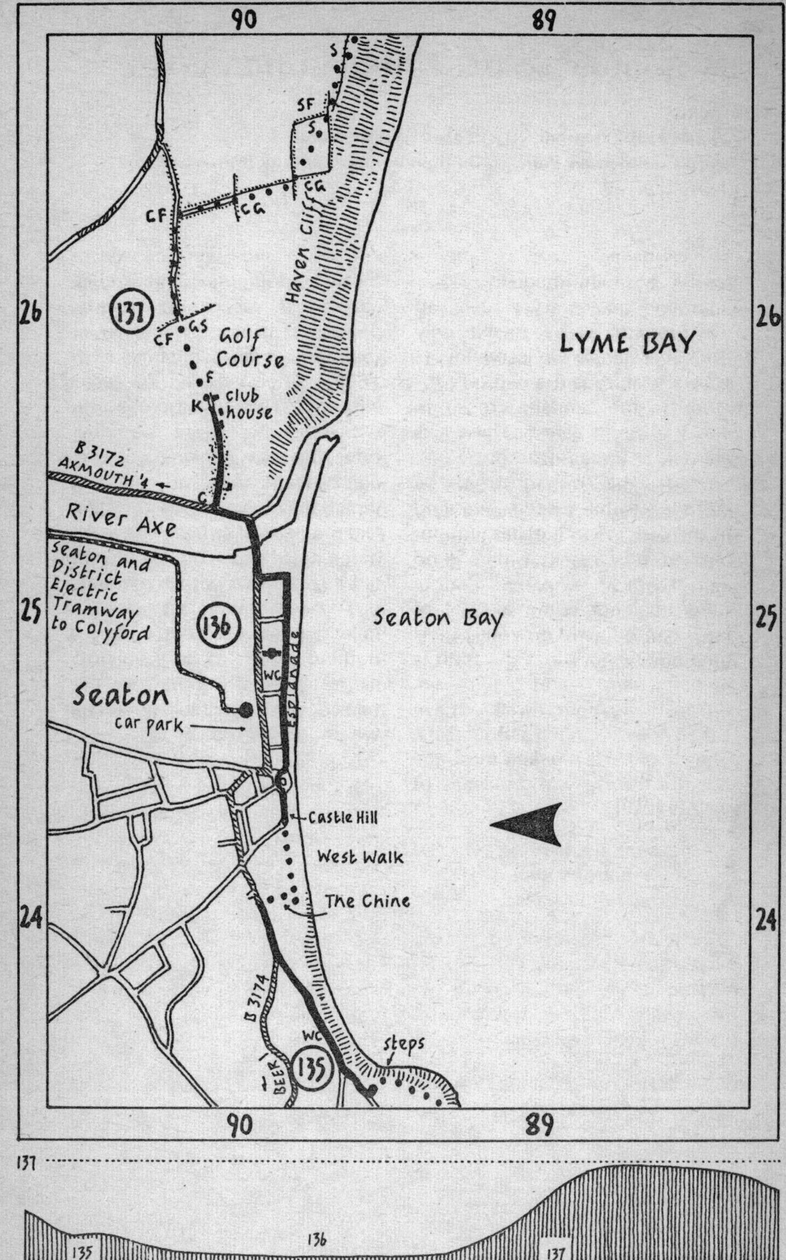

90
89
S
SF
S
CG
Haven Cliff
CF
CG
26
137
26
LYME BAY
CF
GS
Golf
Course
F
K
club
house
B 3172
AXMOUTH '4
River Axe
Seaton and
District
Electric
Tramway
to Colyford
25
136
25
Seaton Bay
WC
Esplanade
Seaton
car park
24
24
Castle Hill
West Walk
The Chine
B 3174
WC
steps
BEER
135
90
89
137
135
136
137

40. Bindon Cliffs, The Landslip

3 miles
Maps: 1:25000 sheet SY29/39; 1:50000 sheet 192
Terrain: Awkward walking along a wooded and overgrown path.

The Landslip is a national nature reserve of much interest to botanists and geologists. Access off the footpath is by permit only from the Nature Conservancy. A special feature is the natural ash-wood in the Landslip cracks, in effect a virgin forest. The rocks are rich in fossils. Do not be discouraged by the notice at the entrance to the reserve, warning of the dangers to life and limb for 5 miles. It is true that there is no exit except at Allhallows School (and this, not being a right of way, can be used only in a genuine emergency) and the Path is in parts narrow and overgrown, but eastward-bound walkers have already passed much sterner tests. The route is waymarked throughout the reserve with splashes of yellow paint.

The landslips were caused by the waterlogging of the chalk causing a succession of slippages, the best known of which took place on Christmas Eve, 1839, when about 20 acres subsided. Two coastguards who witnessed the event described how the sea became violently agitated and how the beach on which they were standing heaved like the deck of a boat. There was much noise and suddenly the cliff fell into the sea with a tremendous roar, forming an island $\frac{3}{4}$ mile long and 60 ft high. There is nothing of this to be seen now, as the action of the sea soon dispersed the unstable material which formed the island.

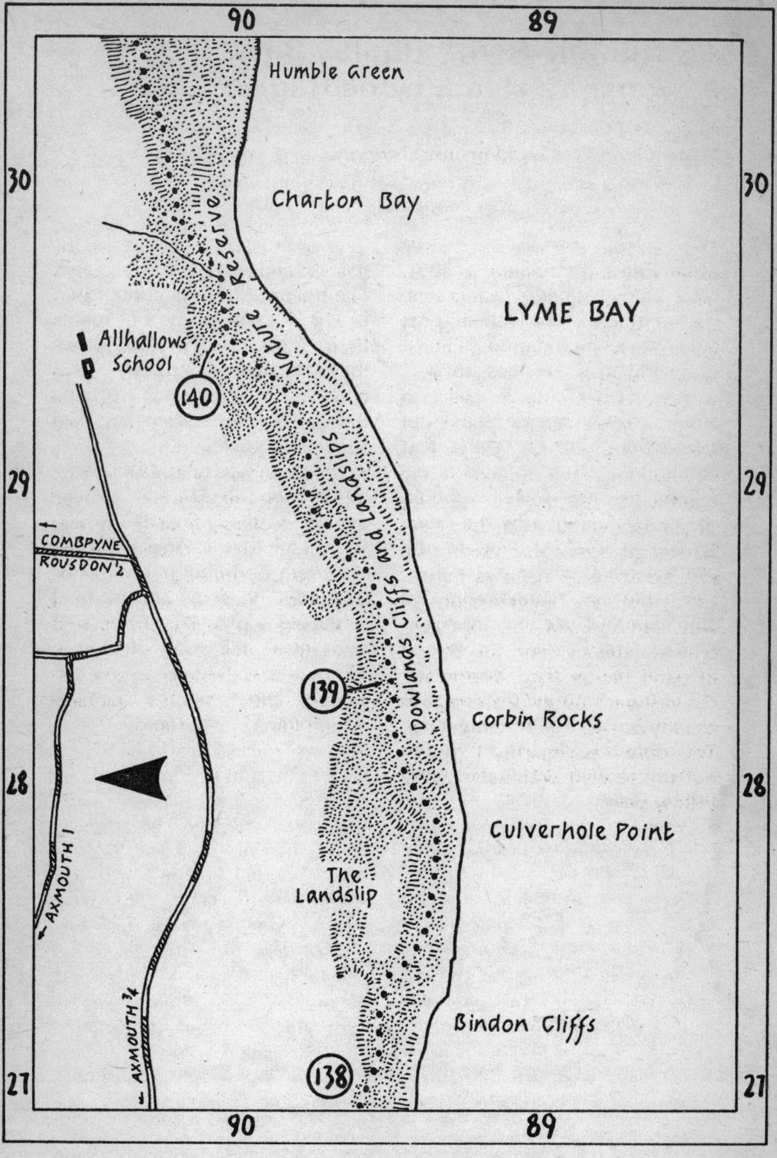

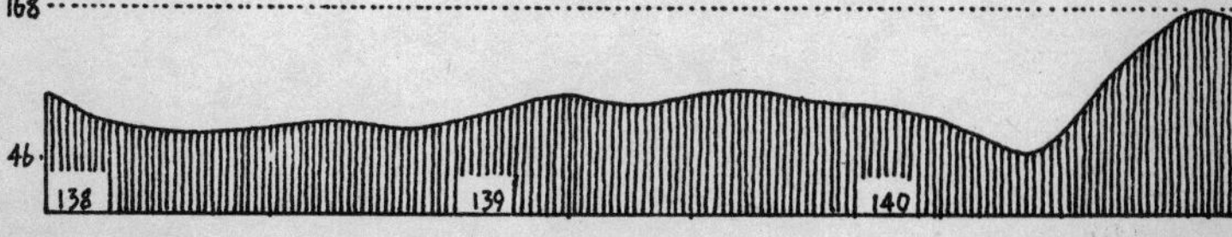

90
89
Humble Green
30
30
Charton Bay
Nature Reserve
LYME BAY
Allhallows
School
140
Dowlands Cliffs and Landslips
29
29
COMBPYNE
ROUSDON 1/2
139
Corbin Rocks
28
28
Culverhole Point
AXMOUTH 1
The
Landslip
AXMOUTH 3/4
Bindon Cliffs
27
138
27
90
89
168
46
138
139
140

41. Humble Point, Pinhay Bay, Devonshire Head, Lyme Regis

3 miles
Maps: 1:25000 sheet SY29/39; 1:50000 sheets 192 and 193
Terrain: An awkward, overgrown section through woods until reaching open fields on the edge of Lyme Regis.

Lyme Regis (population 3,500), has shops, cafés, restaurants, public houses, banks, a post office, accommodation, campsites and bus services to Axminster, Weymouth, Seaton and Sidmouth. Axminster has rail connections to Exeter and London.

West-bound walkers should not be discouraged by the fierce notices at the entrance to the Landslip National Nature Reserve, designed to warn holiday-makers from exploring in court shoes and sandals. The Path is narrow and overgrown, but it is waymarked throughout with yellow splashes of paint. If you cannot manage this section, you must return home, as there is much more arduous walking ahead.

The Cobb, the old stone pier which forms the harbour at Lyme Regis, is lined with quaint shops. There is a marine aquarium on Victoria Pier. The parish church of St Michael the Archangel is mainly sixteenth-century, but the tower dates from the thirteenth century. In a display case in the chancel is a chained copy of a Breeches Bible and a Bad Bible. There is a seventeenth-century gallery and a Jacobean pulpit. The Philpot Museum contains an extensive collection of fossils from the surrounding cliffs, where the study of palaeontology in this country first started. Buddle Bridge is surrounded by old streets and buildings.

The town was granted a charter by Cynewulf in 774 and is mentioned in the Domesday Book. During the Middle Ages it was an important port and in 1347 contributed 4 warships and 62 men to the siege of Calais. Lyme sent two ships to assist in the fight against the Armada, which actually began off the coast at this point. During the Civil War the town was fortified by the parliamentary forces and in 1644 endured a 2-month seige before being relieved by the Earl of Essex. In 1685 the Duke of Monmouth landed on the Cobb in a vain attempt to claim the English throne. Within a few days he had mustered an army of 5,000, but it was a lost cause and after his defeat at Sedgemoor twelve Lyme men who had participated in the rebellion were hanged on the very spot where Monmouth had landed.

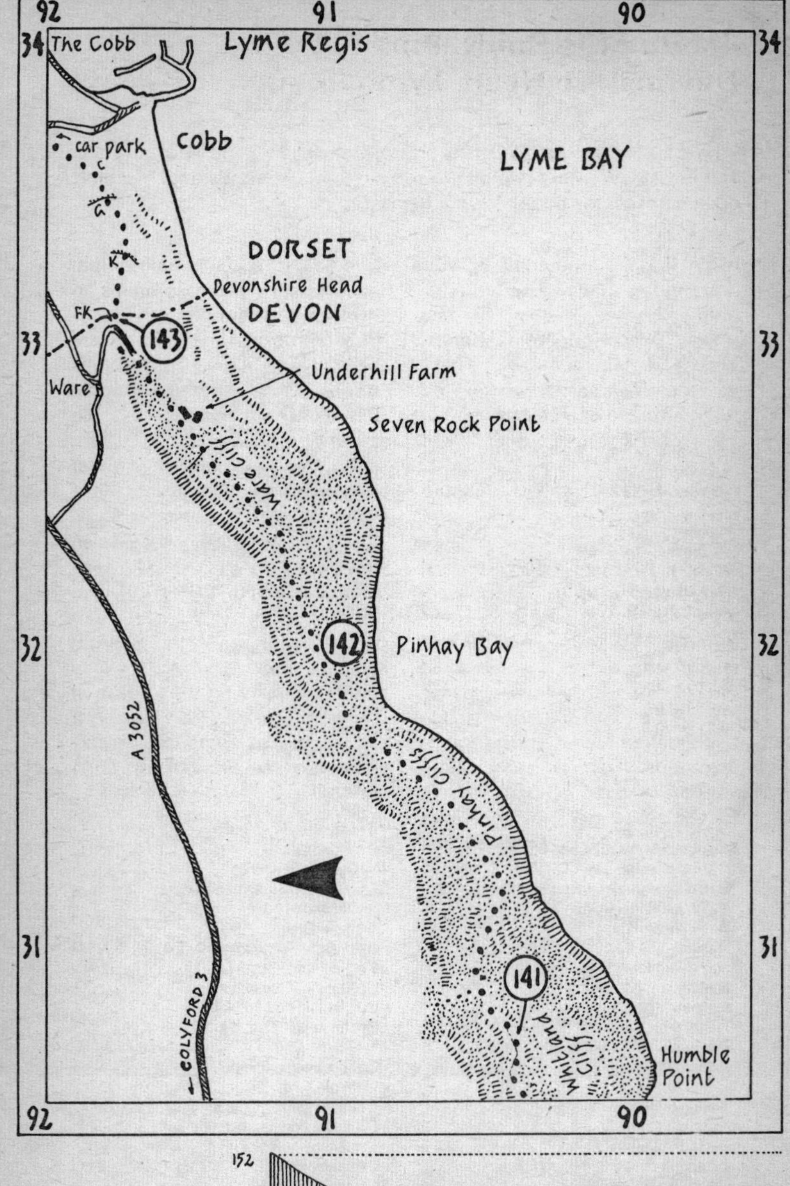
92
91
90
34
The Cobb
Lyme Regis
34
car park
Cobb
LYME BAY
c
G
DORSET
K
Devonshire Head
DEVON
FK
143
33
33
Ware
Underhill Farm
Seven Rock Point
Ware Cliff
32
142
Pinhay Bay
32
A 3052
Pinhay Cliffs
31
31
COLYFORD 3
Whitland Cliffs
141
Humble
Point
92
91
90
152
76
141
142
143

Index of Place Names

Index